21 Days to Enjoying Your Bible

Books in the 21-Day Series

A Proven Plan
for Beginning
New Habits

21 Days to

Enjoying

Your

Bible

Todd Temple

Series Editor Dan Benson

ZondervanPublishingHouse
Grand Rapids, Michigan

A Division of HarperCollinsPublishers

21 Days to Enjoying Your Bible
Copyright © 1998 by Todd Temple

Requests for information should be addressed to:

📖 ZondervanPublishingHouse
Grand Rapids, Michigan 49530

ISBN: 0-310-21745-8

Published in association with the literary agency of Alive Communications, Inc., 1465 Kelly Johnson Blvd., Suite 320, Colorado Springs, CO 80920.

Interior design by Sherri L. Hoffman

Printed in the United States of America

98 99 00 01 02 03 04 /❖ DC/ 10 9 8 7 6 5 4 3

To my friends and partners in the DC/LA conference
ministry of Youth For Christ/USA, whose lives
brightly reflect the Bible's Lead Character.

And we, who with unveiled faces all reflect the Lord's glory, are being transformed into his likeness with ever-increasing glory, which comes from the Lord, who is the Spirit.

—2 Corinthians 3:18

CONTENTS

Part Three: How to Read It

ACKNOWLEDGMENTS

I often tell people that my writing comes not from what I know, but who I know. This book is a testimony to that fact. I am indebted to Melinda Douros, who provided me with simple explanations and clear illustrations for the sections of the Bible that I find most difficult to comprehend; and to Carolyn Poirier, whose love and knowledge of Scripture has helped me in summarizing the books and pointing readers to many delightful verses.

I am thankful to Dan Benson, whose direction and long patience have enabled me to take part in this book line; and to Greg Johnson at Alive Communications, whose constant encouragement and great efforts on my behalf push me to write more clearly with each new work. Above all, I'm thankful for knowing the Author of the great book covered in this little one, for providing a story that's even better in the living than in the reading.

INTRODUCTION

In sixteen years of youth ministry, speaking, and writing, I've heard a lot of troubling questions about the faith: "Why does God allow evil?" "Can you explain the Trinity?" "How can Jesus forgive even people like Hitler?" "Where did God come from?" There are no quick answers to these questions. And the best reply always brings up even more questions.

But the most haunting question I'm asked is answered with a simple yes or no: *"Did you read your Bible today?"*

That one hurts. On most days, I talk about the Bible, or write a study or devotional for the Bible, or quote from the Bible. On many days, I'm promoting the Bible, or producing a commercial for a Bible. And sometimes, at a conference, I even sell a Bible. But *read* it? My answer depends on which day you ask.

So there. I've said it. I struggle with my Bible reading. It's not that I don't have time—I can always make time for what's important. It's not that I don't enjoy reading—books are my favorite sport. And it's certainly not that I can't find one; I've got dozens of them lying around, in three languages, six translations, large print, pocket-sized, leather-bound, and paperback, on CD-ROMs and floppy disks. Finding one is not a problem.

When it comes right down to it, I don't read my Bible daily because I don't *enjoy* it every day. Some days I get to the end of a passage and have no memory of what I just read. Other days I remember it. I just don't understand it. And sometimes, I understand it fine. I just don't believe it. Worst of all is when I believe it, but am too busy, frightened, or pigheaded to do what it says.

Now that I've spilled the truth on my own Bible reading, it's your turn. Do *you* enjoy reading the Bible? Do you wake up each morning saying, "I can't *wait* to crack this book"? As you read, does its message immediately come to life in your head? Do its stories captivate like a good novel, enchant like a classic, and grab your attention like a big news headline? If your answer to these questions is yes, you're excused from this 21-day plan. You pass. Please give this book to a friend!

But if your answer is not so positive—if you struggle with your Bible reading, for whatever reasons—you've come to the right place. This book is for you. And me. And most Christians I know.

YOUR BIBLE-ENJOYMENT HABIT STARTS HERE

Together, we're going to take a whirlwind, 21-day trip through the Bible. We'll visit all the popular stops, as well as a few out-of-the-way places you're going to love. Each day of the trip lasts just 10 to 20 minutes, depending on how fast you read . . . and how many mental pictures you take along the way. You'll need a Bible, a pen, and a readiness to hear God speak to you through his words.

I don't know if you just caught that packing list, so let me repeat the most important item: a Bible. Since the plan here is to help you enjoy *your* Bible, you'll need to bring it along. In fact, if you don't have your Bible open at your side, you'll be lost: With very few exceptions, the verses we look at in *that* book are not printed in *this* one. So you can see how taking this journey without an open Bible would be a real disadvantage, if not pointless.

I use the New International Version when I do quote Scripture here, so if you have a choice, go with NIV for this journey. If you're using another version, that's fine too. Whatever version you use, keep it with you for each lesson. Have I said that enough? Okay, here's the itinerary:

The First Week: What It's Got

Most readers like to stick to their favorite genre—some like romance, others are history buffs; some enjoy poetry, others are adventure addicts; some readers devour self-help books, and others prefer to stick to the news. Whatever your favorite, the Bible's got it.

In the first seven days, I'll show you where to find your kind of writing style . . . and give you tips for enjoying those you may avoid in your other reading choices. By the end of the week, you'll be a connoisseur of your favorite genre and an informed admirer of the rest.

The Second Week: How It's Organized

The best rule for traveling through foreign lands—and foreign literature: *use a map.* We'll take ten days to map out the major sections of the Bible—who wrote them, when, why—and what they tell us about God and his role in our lives. There are seven major Bible sections: the Pentateuch, Historical books, Poetical books, Prophetical books, Gospels and Acts, the Letters, and Revelation.[1] Three of these sections are pretty thick (Historical, Prophetical, Letters), so I've split each of them into two-day adventures. By the end of the ten days, you'll be able to find your way anywhere in the Bible. And on future trips on your own, you'll know what to look for, what to do while you're there, and what to take home with you when you leave.

The Third Week: How to Read It

We'll be tackling tough Bible reading challenges in parts 1 and 2, but I've saved the high hurdles for the end: The things that detour us from our Bibles ... and the things that keep us from applying what it says. In each of the four final days, we'll take on a common complaint about the Bible and show you how to resolve the problem. Four popular complaints, four practical solutions, and a brand-new old book to test them in.

STARTING THE JOURNEY

As I wrap up this introduction, I'm sure I'm supposed to say something like, "If you follow this simple 21-day plan, your Bible-reading struggles will be gone for good." Well there, I said it. But I didn't mean it. Let's face it. The Bible is a *big* book. An *old* book. And it takes on life's deepest and most difficult questions. Mastering its mysteries is not a three-week process. It's a lifelong journey.

This book is just the start. Or maybe for you, more like a refueling stop. In either case, three weeks is just about right. In 21 days, we humans can learn to make a habit out of just about anything. Here's your next habit: Open the Bible and *enjoy* what you read. Let God's Word seep into your head, flow into your heart, and spill out in your thoughts, dreams, words, and deeds.

So give it a try for three weeks. When we visit a Scripture passage, don't just read it. Enjoy it. If it's funny, laugh. If it's sad, be sad. If it's trying to speak to your heart, let it through. And if it does none of the above, find out why. It is, after all, God's Word—a direct message from the Creator, addressed to your heart. The joy is in the catching.

Enough of this chat. By my calculations, it's Day 1 already. Let's get this habit started.

PART ONE

What It's Got

It's Got Pictures

Look for Self-Portraits of God's Character

Does your Bible have photos in it? Mine doesn't. Just some maps in the back. Photography was invented eighteen centuries too late to catch God on film. I'm not complaining, but even a few sketches would have been nice. When God made those spectacular Old Testament appearances, did no one stop and say, "This would look great as a painting"? Maybe they were too busy holding on for dear life. But surely *someone* among Jesus' followers knew how to sketch a likeness. Unfortunately, we have no drawings to prove it.

I miss those pictures. Raised on faded film-strips and flickering TV images, I'm accustomed to seeing images of the really important stuff, like the anatomy of a molecule, and whether Gilligan will ever get off the island. It seems to me that details about God—who he is, what he looks like, what he did—would rank among things most deserving a picture. But he gave us no pictures. Just a bunch of words.

Strike that. Actually, he did give us pictures . . . but he used words to draw them. Like a computer image constructed from thousands of simple pixels, God has painted stunning self-portraits with simple words. One of the most enjoyable Bible pastimes is to connect the words to see these pictures. There are thousands of such portraits—enough to fill an album. They *do*: the Bible is God's photo album.

A CHARACTER STUDY

On every page, God includes a picture of himself: Sometimes it's a larger-than-life portrait. Other times he makes a Hitchcock cameo. And once, on an extended tour of the Holy Land, he let a camera crew document his every move. Look for the self-portrait on each page—it's a telling likeness of his character.

Let's examine some of these character snapshots. We'll start with something big: **Read *Exodus 19:16–19.***

Moses had met with God privately a few times in the past, but this meeting was different. It was open to the public. God made a stunning entrance: a ground-trembling, ear-piercing, smoky descent onto Mount Sinai. Then the Israelites heard God's voice for the first time.

First impressions are important. God knew that. What impression was he trying to make? If you were a reporter in that crowd, jotting down notes of your first impression of God, what would you have written? My notes might have looked like this:

Big!
Loud!
Powerful!
Scary!

After the dust had settled and my heart rate returned to normal, I might also have jotted down this note: "Moses is someone special." That's clearly what God wanted everyone to think. He wanted people to know that Moses was his man, his mouthpiece, his chosen deputy. But even that fact is a telling reflection of God's own character. He chooses mere humans to speak for him. That's a hint. God paints self-portraits on the faces of men and women. More on that in a bit.

Seeking and discovering God-portraits makes reading the Bible more enjoyable. It's even more fun when you find a picture God liked so much that he recycled parts of it to use later in the book. This Exodus passage contains a few of those popular parts. The first one shows up in verse 16: "On the morning of the third day, there was thunder and lightning." The "third day" gives it away.

When Jesus was making the disciples nervous with talk of his imminent death, he told them he would be raised up "on the third day." His allusion to the past became the ultimate proof of his deity: When the morning of the third day rolled by, so did the stone. God began his last public appearance . . . until his encore. But now we're really getting ahead of the story.

One more comment about the Exodus picture. The writer of Hebrews recycles it to compare the unapproachable God of Mount Sinai to the embraceable Jesus of Mount Zion (Hebrews 12:18–24). Two awesome pictures of the same God. In the first, he's bigger than life. In the second, he's bigger than death. That's big.

CAMEOS OF GOD

Most people are familiar with God's big pictures. They've read these stories or seen Hollywood's reenactments on the big screen. The jumbo-size portraits are popular because they're so stunning. But God doesn't often make big pictures of himself. He saves those for special occasions. Most of his biblical portraits are subtle. Read too closely and you lose them in the details. Read too fast and you miss them altogether. The trick is to read like you're looking for God. See what he looks like in this next passage. **Read *Hosea 11:1–9*.**

Stop for a moment. Did you *really* look up the verse in your own Bible? If you did, you're free to go. Jump down to the next paragraph while I talk to the troublemakers. Okay, I don't want to sound like a pest, but *you're* the one who bought this book. *You're* the one who wants to increase your Bible-reading enjoyment. You can't do that if you don't jump in there and get acquainted (or reacquainted). What's thirty seconds between friends? Rejoin us after you've had your visit with Hosea.

When I read a verse like this, I get distracted by the names. Who's *Admah*? Who's *Zebolim*? But we're not playing that game right now. Nor are we exploring history or prophecy, so we don't have to hunt down a "return to Egypt" or a trip back from Assyria. We're just looking for God. When that's our goal, he's easy to spot.

Among the many illustrations here, we find God as a loving, exasperated parent. He's poured his love into his child, yet "the more I called Israel, the further they went from me." As every parent knows, you can't force your children to love you. You do everything you can to prepare them for the world, warn them of its dangers, and prove your undying love for them, but sometimes they just don't get it. Clearly, God can relate.

WHEREFORE'S WALDO?

Searching for pictures of God is kind of like flipping through a *Where's Waldo?* book. You know he's on the page somewhere; you just have to find him. But there's more to it than that. No one stops to ask *why* Waldo is on the page. Once you find him, you flip the page. That's not how you play *Where's God?*

The Bible is an intentional book; God had a *reason* for including each portrait. As soon as you've spotted a picture, you must ask *why* he included it in the collection. What is God trying to tell us about himself? What part of his character is he revealing to us?

Let's consider the Hosea passage above. Why does God want us to see him as a parent? Why is this view of such importance that he made sure it got placed in the Bible? Or to put it another way: How would we act if we *didn't* see him as a parent? If Exodus 19 were our only snapshot, we'd surely fear him, knowing that he could strike us dead for deserting him. But Hosea shows us a God whose heart *breaks* when we run from him. Our sin doesn't just disappoint, offend, and anger him. It *grieves* him. It *hurts* him. It arouses his *compassion*.

When we see God in this light, our relationship changes. And so it happens with every new view of God. God placed self-portraits in the Bible so we could get to know him better and better with each turn of the page.

IN HIS IMAGE

Let's review. Step 1: When you read the Bible, don't just look for who did what and when; look for God's self-portraits. Step 2: When you spot a picture of God, don't just turn the page to look for the next one. Stop and ask *why* God chose to place this view of himself in the Bible. Each picture is an act of self-disclosure. God opens up and shows us who he really is, so we can grow closer to him.

One more step: Copy the picture! God did not copyright his portraits. On the contrary, he *wants* us to reproduce them—in our own character. He's already drawn the outline sketch: We've been created in his image. What's more, we're *still* being sketched into his image. Every day. The last part of 2 Corinthians 3:18 (TLB) puts it this way: "As the spirit of the Lord works within us, we become more and more like him." So search for

God's self-portraits as you read. Take a good look—you might just look like that yourself someday.

LESSON OF THE DAY

Look for self-portraits of God's character— then copy the pictures.

It's Got Adventure

Join God on a New Adventure Today

For Someone who's the pinnacle of patience, God sure doesn't sit around much. It seems he's always up to some new adventure . . . and that usually means he's taking along others for the ride. Through imagination, we can join his old journeys.

But beware. If you're a fan of adventure stories, you may be disturbed by God's idea of adventure. Most modern adventures share comfortably predictable features: A reluctant hero encounters the villain and is defeated . . . for a time. Hero and villain struggle through the bulk of the story, then things get a whole lot worse before they finally get better. And they always get better—the hero always wins in the end.

At least it's that way in my favorite stories: In *The Hobbit*, Bilbo saves the day. In *The Lion, the Witch and the Wardrobe*, Aslan and the children put an end to winter's wicked witch. Humphrey prevails over *The Sea-Wolf*, and

David Balfour escapes in *Kidnapped*. Each story is moral, inspiring . . . and predictable. I like them that way.

I guess that's why I'm disturbed by so many Bible stories. I expect them to follow the same pattern. They're in the Bible, after all—don't they have to be moral and inspiring? Apparently not, because God's adventures often contain implausible encounters, evil left unpunished, and occasionally, a dead hero.

Then there's the blood and gore—fratricide, genocide, suicide, adultery, prostitution, rape, child molestation, animal cruelty, and environmental devastation. A true depiction of the Bible on film would get an "R" rating. This is not a collection of adventure stories for children. Nor is it an easy read for the rest of us.

GOD'S IDEA OF ADVENTURE

We can read the Bible two ways: for what it says or for what we expect it to say. Most people expect Bible stories to be soft and cuddly, moral and inspiring, with triumphantly happy endings. When they come upon a story that doesn't match their expectations, they skip it, disbelieve it, or just give up and catch a rerun of *Little House on the Prairie*. But those who read it for what it says are in for a wild ride.

Let's take one of those rides now. Get ready, it's a slippery one. **Read *Genesis 32:22–30*.**

This story is downright strange, and no easy moral lies there. If you're up for your own adventure, try telling it to a classroom of sixth graders. Their questions will eat you alive: If that's really God in the wrestling match, what's he doing in human form? Why doesn't God just pin Jacob in the first three seconds and call it a night? What's God doing rolling around in the dirt? Isn't that a bit undignified for the Creator and King of the universe?

Fast-talking Sunday school teachers may weasel their way out of such questions, but they'll miss the message if they do. If it is indeed God that Jacob's wrestling with, then it is our own story: We wrestle with God. For proof, look at round one—the story you just read! If you asked some of the same questions those sixth graders did . . . if you're saying to yourself, "How can this story be true?" . . . if you're trying hard to believe what seems unbelievable . . . then you too are trying to wrap your arms around a God who's not so easy to grasp. And God himself pulled you straight into the struggle.

HEROES LOSE

Wrestling with God in his stories takes courage because the match usually ends in our own defeat. Look at the box scores: Abraham throws in the towel by agreeing to sacrifice his own son at God's request. Jonah makes no high-seas escape—the fish "gives it up" only after Jonah does. Mary, the most blessed among women, gives birth to a child she knows she's going to lose. And Jesus accepts execution for a crime he never committed.

In each of these stories, there's no ingenious battle plan, no brilliant escape, no just deserts for the villain. There's the hero's defeat, and God's victory.

Ready for another disturbing adventure? **Read *Deuteronomy 32:48–52.***

At just three months of age, Moses takes a Nile river cruise . . . in a basket. Pharaoh's daughter finds and adopts him, and he grows up to a life brimming with the things that make for a great story. He leads the Israelites out of slavery and into a roundabout, 40-year trek through the desert. Through most of the adventure, Moses is on a first-name basis with God and meets with him often. He's clearly God's hero.

But when he's one river away from the Promised Land, God puts an end to his wild ride. Moses dies in sight of the goal he was born to complete. All because of something he did decades earlier. (For the details of the offending incident, you can read Numbers 20:1–13.)

Here's the short version: The Israelites are raising a ruckus because they're thirsty. God tells Moses to lift that famous staff and speak to a rock, which will gush with water on command. As the people gather around the rock to see what's going to happen, Moses rebukes them: "Must we bring you water from this rock?"—as if he were the provider, not God. Then he *hits* the rock with the staff. That was not in the instructions. The water bursts out, which is tasty for the Israelites, an image-booster for Moses, and a slap in God's face.

Moses had his victory then and there. As we learned earlier, that's not how God works. In *his* adventures, the happy endings come through the hero's surrender and defeat.

Wait, I see a hand up. "Why didn't God forgive Moses and let him go into the Promised Land?" Well, God *did* forgive him—the two continued to have face-to-face meetings (without forgiveness, these would have been face-to-crispy-corpse meetings), and God kept blessing Moses and guiding the people toward their goal. But the damage had been done. In front of everyone, Moses dishonored God. And very soon, the rest of the Israelites did the same thing. God forgives sins, but he doesn't turn back time and erase the consequences. So when it came time for Israel's next big adventure, God raised up another leader. Joshua took over and led the Israelites across the Jordan goal line.

I see another hand. "If the cost of faithfully following God is *defeat*, what's the point of following him?" Good question. Here's the strange answer: *The defeats are temporary and always lead to a bigger victory.* Before I explain that, let me give you an analogy. I have to switch from adventure story to war story here, so don't wander off.

In every war, the general must fight at least two battles. The first battle is over the hearts of the soldiers, who must surrender their personal whims to the will of their commander. The second battle is the one they fight *together*.

And so it is with God. In the first battle, we must surrender our selfish, independent ways to him. When our allegiance is clear, he can proceed with the ultimate battle against the Enemy ... and we can take part in that victory. Our personal defeats are temporary, but *necessary* for ultimate victory. Of course, in this war God's going to win with or without us, but the thrill is in joining him, not in winning the skirmishes against him along the way.

End of war analogy. Let's return to the adventure. God is the Guide, and the first thing he wants to know is, Will you follow him, or wander off on your own misadventure? He'll let you choose either path, but his way is better.

HOW TO PACK

If you want to enjoy the Bible's adventure stories, you've got to take them as they are. God makes no promises that they'll be easy, fun, inspiring, or immediately victorious. That's because they're *real life* adventures, and he makes no guarantees about life either. Except one. If you want to win, you must *give up*. If you want to be first, make yourself last. If you want to survive life's journey, cancel all your travel plans and follow him. He— and only he—knows the way.

This outrageous strategy works for your Bible reading too. There's a *reason* for these stories. God is trying to show you something. And you won't spot it unless you're willing to follow where he leads. Put away your ideas about how the stories *ought* to go. Set aside your criticism and incredulity; throw away your comforting conclusions. Unbuckle your safety belt, grab God's hand and hang on for dear life.

Here's the scariest part: The God who took the ancients on these adventures is still leading treks today. He has another trip departing now. The details are sketchy, but based on the accounts of previous adventurers, you can expect difficulty, danger, fear, exhaustion—and if the Guide has his way, defeat.

This much is certain: Whatever journey he takes you on today will prepare you for even greater adventures in your future.

LESSON OF THE DAY

Join God on a new adventure today—
unbuckle your safety belt, grab God's hand,
and hang on for dear life.

It's Got Romance

Fall in Love Today

The Bible is rich in romance ... *if* you're willing to broaden your definition a bit. Nowadays, the word *romance* conjures up visions of first kisses and prom dates, candlelit trysts and courtship ... real or wished for. In short, we use the word to describe the feelings and experiences of being in love.

Romance hasn't always been so narrowly defined. Originally, romances were medieval stories (written in a Roman dialect, hence the name) recounting the real-life adventures of knights: tales of chivalry, honor, duty, patriotism, sacrifice. They were still about love—passionate acts done in the name of faith, truth, country, and clan.

In this broader sense, the Bible is unquestionably romantic. Its best stories overflow with passion: Moses kills an Egyptian caught abusing a slave; Hannah gives up baby Samuel to honor a pact with God; Ruth abandons home and country to faithfully follow her mother-in-law; Daniel risks execution to obey a Higher

Court; Esther foils a plot to kill the Jews; Stephen is martyred while preaching the painful truth.

These stories—and dozens more—fit the broader definition of romance. Each moves the reader to empathy, anger, longing, indignation, or celebration. We *feel* the stories deep down in the place where our values and emotions collide. That's real romance, and the Bible delivers it in hearty measure.

But what about the more modern definition of romance—the acts and emotions of a man and woman in love? The Bible has fewer such stories, and they're very short. In Genesis 29 you'll find Jacob and Rachel ... make that Jacob and Leah, *then* Rachel. Together (and with the help of their maids Bilhah and Zilpah) they become the parents of the twelve tribe-starting sons and the very-great-grandparents of an entire nation. Nine centuries later there's another famous love story. Ruth *isn't* one of Jacob's descendants, but in the book bearing her name she joins the ancient family, through a curious, threshing-floor courtship with Boaz that leads to marriage, motherhood, and eventually, a royal dynasty.

The most famous boy-meets-girl story is Song of Songs, which tells of Solomon's courtship and marriage to one of his many wives. Depending on your imagination in metaphor, it's either a squeaky clean love poem or a diary of erotic adventure. (Personally, I've never gotten far with the "teeth like a flock of sheep" line, but maybe that's just me.)

You'll find lots of romance in the Bible, and a few great love stories. But they're nothing compared to the greatest love story, which uses the entire Bible in the telling.

GOD'S LOVE STORY

God is a romantic, first to last. He's *got* to be—he's the definition of love itself. The Bible tells his romance: He's the faithful lover; we are his unfaithful beloved. From Genesis to Revelation, we catch him in spectacular acts of love. And in the same space, we read about humans who spurn his love to embrace other "gods" they think are better, but who turn out to be a whole lot worse.

The best illustration of this on-again, off-again romance is given in the book of Hosea. At first glance, it's the story of a nice boy named Hosea, a bad girl named Gomer, and their children whose names are stranger than their parents'. After a short stint as wife, Gomer returns to her previous career: prostitution. To catch what happens next, **read Hosea 3:1–3**.

Hosea has every right to forsake his adulterous wife. Instead, he redeems her by paying off the pimp and bringing her home. It's a startling tale of fidelity and unstoppable love. But it gets better. Take a closer look and you see the *other* love story: a faithful lover named God, a faithless nation called Israel, and their rebellious children. After the honeymoon, Israel forsakes God and returns to her adulterous ways. Instead of abandoning her to destruction, God redeems Israel and carries her back to himself.

That's exactly what God has done for all of us in Jesus. He has redeemed us, buying us back from destruction with his own blood. We were like Gomer—prostitutes, unfaithful, selfish pursuers of other gods. But God paid the price to bring us home. Now we can live forever with him.

The New Testament returns to this marriage metaphor again and again. Jesus is bridegroom, the church his bride. A successful marriage demands open communication, commitment, obedience, discipline, respect, and forgiveness. That's how God treats us, and he expects us to return the gesture. When we *don't*—when we're unfaithful, uncaring, unthankful—God's love compels him to pursue us again. He's unstoppable.

FALLING IN LOVE

The Bible's great history, prophecy, theology, and practical advice are all helpful and important, worthy of careful reading. But don't let the facts, figures, and helpful living tips distract you from the point of it all. What's the value in reading the stories and commandments and sermons if all they do is point us to a God who hates us—or doesn't care about us one way or another? Who wants to spend eternity with an enemy, grouch, or Apathetic Force? If that's what's in store for us in the eternal realm, we can dispense with Bible reading and start grabbing whatever we want in life *now*, because it goes downhill from here.

Thank God that's not true. It's precisely because God *loves* us that this book matters at all. The Bible is God's great love story, written to show us a relentless, passionate, unquenchable Lover who stops at nothing to prove his love.

Remember this overriding love theme when you open your Bible. Let your heart pound as you read his great acts of love. Feel it break when you see his love spurned. Rejoice when you witness a reunion. Cheer when you watch God and his people walking hand in hand. And every once in a while, pause in your reading and thank him for marrying you.

LESSON OF THE DAY

*Fall in love today. Let your heart pound
as you ponder a God who stops
at nothing to love you.*

It's Got Poetry

*Use Your Head and Heart to Form What
You Can't See or Hear*

God wants to show us things that cannot be seen, tell us things our ears cannot hear. Not a problem. He's given us a head and heart that can be directed to sculpt clear *forms* out of intangible ideas. It's a sculpting trick he uses himself—only when *he* does it, the forms become *real*. Take a look at some of his journal entries: *"Day 1: 'Let there be light'—light becomes real."* *"Day 124,530,048,224,990,374,444,182,395,571: 'Let there be Todd'—Todd becomes real."* (Okay, so I made up that last part. But you get the point.)

Our own word powers aren't so great. Our forms don't become real in that sense, but they do come to life in our mind. We perceive the idea as if we could see and hear it. That's how poetry works. The poet combines words that, in the right combinations, sculpt forms in our minds.

The Bible is filled with such poetry. Indeed, the entire book forms an epic poem, brimming with ideas we can't actually see or hear, but can *know* nonetheless. When we read God's poetry, we must see and hear it not with eyes and ears, but with head and heart.

Let's try that now. Turn to the first stanza: *Genesis 1:1–5*.

Like all great poetry, this piece both fulfills and transcends its purpose. It matters that we know God created the world, that he brought light from darkness. But we can begin to understand this truth only when we experience him doing the same thing in our own lives—bringing light out of our own darkness, brooding like a mother hen over the face of our own death-like deep.

Maybe that's why we have such a hard time explaining the creation story to those who want a sanitized, play-by-play account. If we stray too far from the poetry, we lose our own sense of the experience. We *know* God created the world that way because we've seen him do a similar work in our hearts. But how can something cataclysmic be so sublime, so unexplainable? We can try to understand this act of creation with scopes, computers, and 3-D animations, and in the end our model lays there dead like a fish on the beach.

God doesn't use poetry to sidestep science or to obscure the truth. Nor is he after some cosmic creative-writing award. When God chooses poetry, he does so because it's the best way to show us something we cannot know through eyes and ears. The Poet wants to give us a living picture, not a dead fish. To prove it, he begins his Book that way.

And as it turns out, he's just getting started. Thousands of stanzas later, God recalls the opening lines of his great poem to announce the next grand moment in Creation. **Read *John 1:1–14*.**

"The Word"—the Poem, the Picture—"became flesh and made his dwelling among us." In the creation account, God paints a picture we can see only in our hearts. In John 1, he paints himself into the picture so he can *live* in our hearts.

We can come up with all sorts of fancy diagrams and detailed descriptions to convey the stunning connection between these two events, but nothing we devise will make it clearer than the poetry we've been given. So let's move on.

Just as the Word spoke the universe into being, he spoke *us* into being. Did you catch that? We're not the result of accidental, random acts of unconscious forces. Each of us is "real" because the Poet wrote us into existence. We have that fact in writing. **Check out *Ephesians 2:10*.**

The Greek word for "workmanship" is *poema*. Try reading the verse that way: "We are God's *poema.* . . ." Each of us is a deliberate, carefully crafted work of God, come to life in the power of his poetic skills. Each is an authentic, original composition, arranged by the master Poet himself. He even signed his work with an indelible mark: his own image. More on this personal poem in a moment.

Let's get back to the biblical poem. Jump to the end and **read *Revelation 22:13*.**

Okay, so it's not the *very* end, but it's close. To ears familiar with the bluster and boast of movie ads, prize fighters, and political tyrants, this verse sounds like hyperbole. But God is simply stating the facts. He's the frame around the painting he's been showing us since the start—there's nothing outside the picture, nothing before or after himself. He's "the beginning and the end."

How else could God describe what he knows is beyond our experience? Everything in our world has a beginning—we celebrate these inceptions with birthdays and New Years and Fourth of July. Things *begin* because other things that existed before them—parents and orbits and colonists—gave them their start. But God has no birthday—he *is* the beginning.

God is not merely the first letter in the alphabet of the universe, he's also the last. That's just as hard to comprehend: Everything in our experience has an ending—recorded in time, tombstone, or textbook, by something or someone who happens to have a later expiration date. God has no such date in his future. He *is* the end. And since that's an important, albeit incomprehensible, fact, he uses poetry to convey it.

POETRY RECITAL

We've just taken four trips into Scripture, yet not one of them landed in the Poetical books. I did that to show you the extent of God's poetry. It really does span the Bible; you'll find examples in nearly every book.

For good reason: Unlike us, the ancient Jews had no written Bible within reach. Reading the Scriptures was a privilege reserved for religious leaders. For most folk, God's Word was something to be heard, sung, and memorized. Poetry is especially suited for these purposes, so the biblical writers used it often.

We can be thankful that their poetry doesn't rely on rhyme or syllabic rhythm, which would all be lost in the translation. In the main, the writers used more transportable techniques to compose their verses, ensuring that patterns and meanings would read and sound well in most any language.

Their favorite trick was parallelism, repeating words or restating ideas from line to line. This allows the words themselves to drive the rhythm—whether heard in Hebrew or English, Urdu or Armenian. Some lines cascade through synonymous ideas, others are antithetical (contrasting ideas). These and other forms of parallelism lead the reader or listener into a loose cadence; stress the right words and it almost seems to rhyme.[1]

A technique that gets left behind when you translate out of the Hebrew is acrostic construction. In it the writer uses the alphabet to build the poem. In Psalm 119, there are 22 stanzas, one for each letter of the Hebrew alphabet. Each of the eight lines in a stanza begins with the same letter. The poem reads just fine without the acrostic—in fact, trying to translate it into our alphabet just messes it up.

Acrostic construction is also used in Lamentations. In both of these instances, the English translation is plenty powerful without alphabetical arrangement, so no need to rush out and learn Hebrew, unless you're a purist.

READ WITH HEAD AND HEART

There's a lot more to poetry than I've covered here. If you're a poet or a student of poetry, you're wondering how I could have left it all out. But if you are such a person, then you probably already enjoy reading the Bible's poetry, so you can just jump in and play away. For the rest of us—those who slept through poetry lessons in school, who seldom caught what others saw clearly—the poetry in the Bible can be a challenge to understand and enjoy.

Here's the key: When you read a piece of God's poetry, don't squint! Maybe there's a complicated pattern in there somewhere—an ingenious construction of meter and mathematics that boggles the imagination. So what? God speaks just fine without a metronome. Maybe there's a deeper metaphor, buried beneath three similes, two analogues, and a paradigm. Don't sweat it—leave something to discover on a future visit.

Instead, sit back and let the words form pictures in your head and heart. Imagine God as painter, your mind the canvas. What do the words *look* like, *sound* like, *feel* like? If reading and perceiving at the same time is tough for you (it is for me sometimes), close your eyes and listen to the words: Read a verse, then stop and ponder; ask someone to read it to you; get an audio recording of the Bible; or record your own reading and play it as you drive. (Careful with this last one; certain poetical sections of Revelation may cause you to swerve uncontrollably.)

Remember that for most of history, the majority didn't read God's poetry at all. They *listened* to it. It was written for aural consumption . . . and still goes down best when administered through the ears.

LESSON OF THE DAY

Use your head and heart to form what you can't see or hear—and let God continue his work today in forming you.

It's Got Reality

Read It Like a Newspaper

If the criteria for writing a good religious book include the requirement that it must be ethereal, unearthly, and pristine, God failed big-time. The Bible is not just an account of life the way it *should* be, or *will* be when we finally land in heaven. It's about life, the way it *is*: love and hate, peace and violence, kindness and abuse, blood, intrigue, hope, betrayal, sex, laughter, mystery, murder, and sacrifice. If you were to change the names to protect the ancient, many sections would read like today's news . . . or this week's tabloid.

Here's an example. **Read 2 Samuel 11:2–5.**[1]

This royal scandal would make the cover of *Newsweek* if it weren't for the fact that it happened 3,000 years ago. And just like modern royalty, David would have landed on the cover again with a follow-up story. Read verses 14 through 17.

In an effort to cover his adulterous tracks, David brings Uriah home from the war. It's a good plan: Uriah will have sex with his wife, then think she's carrying his own child. But Uriah goes and spoils it all by refusing to go to his house. He tells David he can't sleep with his wife while his soldiers are deprived of their own home privileges. Time for a new plan. You just read it.

And that's what's most remarkable about this story. *It made it into print.* A scandal's not a scandal till the public finds out about it. Until then, it's *just a sin* (that's an oxymoron, but you get the point). Nowadays, it's pretty tough for the famous or powerful to keep their sins out of the news. But surely God could have buried *this* story—he was the only publisher!

If you're a news hound, you're already asking the next question: Why did God publish a story that besmirches the character of one of his greatest followers? That's the story behind the story: the *reason* this story was released to the public. Let's explore it.

What did God have to gain by its release? As we learned in Day 1, he uses the text to reveal pictures of his own character. David's sins don't do that. But not even King David can stand in the way of God when he wants to make an appearance. By publishing this story, God shows us he's a reliable, impartial reporter of the truth. We can have confidence in the veracity of his words. That's nice to know when we stumble upon the *other* kind of story—the one that *seems* too good to be true.

If the publication of the story is a reflection of God's character, the *facts* are a reflection of our own. Even the best and brightest and most godly among us are not immune to sin. David's actions are proof that God is not an option, but a necessity. You'll have to read further in the story to hear about Nathan's blistering rebuke and the king's painful restoration to God's grace. But the lesson is clear: If this king-adulterer-murderer can find forgiveness, there's hope for you and me.

The story of David and Bathsheba reads like today's news because all its key elements are timeless. Adultery has not gone out of style. Murder is as popular as ever. The rich, the power-ful, and the godly still fall. But most importantly, the God who forgave sin back then is still in business today. This is not an ancient story or a current event. It's reality for all time.

And that's the trick: Read it that way. This stuff *happened*. And like it or not, it's *still* happening, all around us, everywhere you look.

NOT JUST REAL NEWS
BUT GOOD NEWS

Unlike most news media, which recount the problems, dig up the dirt, and uncover the scandals in our world, the Bible offers *solutions*. Not pie-in-the-sky, by-and-by platitudes, but real answers to life's most pernicious ills.

Paul's letters to the churches deliver this kind of news. He's not afraid to report the dirty truth. But he always follows up with solution coverage. **Read** his news column in *1 Corinthians 5:1–2*.

He doesn't name names, but his readers know who he's talk-ing about. Just look for the church member who's shacked up with his stepmom. If Paul had stopped the story there, he'd be just another gossip columnist, teasing the sordid attentions of his readers. But he moves quickly from problem to solution. Read verse 11.

It's simple: When a church member persists in his sinful lifestyle, take him off the welcome list. Problem, solution. Paul reveals his Publisher's simple news policy in another letter. **Check out** *Ephesians 5:11–14.*

It's all about dark and light. Use the light of God's truth to expose the problems hidden in the darkness. The entire Bible is written according to this policy. Nathan exposed David's dark sins to the light of God's truth. Paul's reports to the churches follow the same policy. Darkness, light. Hidden, revealed. Real problem, real solution.

Since that's the way the Bible is written, that's how we should read it. First look for the bad news. (You don't have to look very hard.) Then see if it looks suspiciously similar to a story in your own life. If it looks familiar—and unfortunately, it often does—then keep reading till you get to the good news. Chances are, the solution will work for you today as well as it did back then.

That's because the Publisher of this news is the only one with the perspective to offer real solutions to life's real problems, then and now.

LESSON OF THE DAY

Read the Bible like a newspaper, written by Someone who delivers real solutions to today's real problems.

It's Got History

Relive the Best Parts

The Bible is the most comprehensive compilation of ancient history we've got, detailing one culture's political, social, economic, and religious life over a 3000-year span. For students of ancient history, it's a treasure of names and places, facts and figures. But the history in the Bible is not just for historians to enjoy. There's great stuff here for all of us. That's because the Bible is no ordinary history book.

Ancient history seldom covers the lifestyles of the poor and unknown. It's written by the rich and powerful, the educated, the literate— the ones who have leisure time to write it down, or money to hire someone to do it for them. Of course they stick to what they know.

Not so with the Bible. It's filled with the details of life outside the palace, beyond the guarded gates, on the other side of the tracks. We've got stories of sheep herders and soldiers, servants and slaves, and an uncommon carpenter from the hicktown of Nazareth. The upper classes have a wealth of history to revel in. The Bible covers the lives of people the rest of us can relate to.

EXPERIMENTING WITH HISTORY

If the Bible were merely ancient history, it would simply be *interesting* (to some of us, anyway). But because it's *repeatable* history, containing important information about how to interact with a living God, it's more than interesting—it's essential.

The three main characters in this ancient history are still alive: God, humans, Satan. Which means we can reenact the stories ourselves. But it's no mere dramatic reenactment. It's a real-life *experiment*: We re-*search* the lives of those who took part in the original experiment (call it "God-human interaction"), and see if we can duplicate the results.

Stephen Hawking describes how this process is used in science to test a theory: "Each time new experiments are observed to agree with the predictions, the theory survives, and our confidence is increased; but if ever a new observation is found to disagree, we have to abandon or modify the theory."

Consider for a moment that the Bible proposes *theories* on who God is and how we are to relate with him. If so, then each day of our lives is an experiment to test these theories. When our own results agree with the findings recorded in the Bible, we have greater confidence in this Book and the theories it proposes.

God knew there would be skeptics among us. Therefore he gave us good data and dares us to test it in our own lives. The "theories" about God and our relationship to him hold up, test after test, person to person, century through century. It's little wonder that many of the most outspoken opponents become the church's most persuasive proponents. From St. Paul to C. S. Lewis to Josh McDowell, we find skeptics who tested the ancient theories and wound up proving themselves wrong.

Wait a minute. A moment ago, we were discussing history. Now we're talking about theories and experiments. Haven't we gotten off track? Not really. Here's where these subjects collide. The Bible records the *history* of these experiments. Hebrews provides us with a prime example. Read the first verse of Hebrews 11.

The writer has just stated a "theory" about faith. Then he offers a volume of historical data, compiled through dozens of famous experiments, to back up the theory. Read verse 2, then quickly skim the rest of the chapter and finish with the first two verses of chapter 12.

While you were skimming, did you catch all the instances of the phrase, "by faith"? Each one announces the results of someone's experiment in that field. The writer concludes the list of historical experiments (performed by a "great cloud of witnesses") with a challenge to conduct our own experiment—or as he puts it, to run the race set before us.

TODAY'S EXPERIMENT

The history contained in the Bible is put there as a record of past inquiries in faith. Why? So we don't have to start from scratch in our own faith experiments. We can read the results of previous inquirers. We can reenact their best experiments to see if we can duplicate their best results.

So today, don't just read this old history, *relive* it, by conducting a self-experiment. Research an old faith experiment and reenact the procedure in your own life. See if the God who proved himself to the ancients will prove himself to you right now.

For example, read Hebrews 11 and take note of the various experiments in faith. Then perform your own faith experiment today: Perform an act of obedience, discipline, forgiveness, mercy, or personal sacrifice, relying not on your own ability, skill, or wealth, but solely on your faith. (Hint: That means pushing yourself beyond the ordinary.) Do something that can only be attributed to God.

For that matter, read the original data for one of the experiments cited in the Hebrews passage—or any other old experiment in faith. Caution: Don't become distracted by the miracles or appearances by God himself. Keep your eye on the *human* part of the equation. What did the test subject do *in faith*? That is, what did he or she do, not for personal gain or selfish glory but strictly in response to God's call, for God's glory? Then act in the same way today.

One more thing: Publish your findings by telling others what happened. They'll want to verify the results in their own lives. Together, you'll form a new cloud of witnesses—a fresh stack of data that proves the theories about God and what he's up to.

LESSON OF THE DAY

Relive the best parts: reenact a great faith experiment in your own life today.

It's Got Practical Advice

For Best Results, Apply Directly

The all-time best-selling self-help book is the Bible. Yet most people wouldn't think of putting this old book on *that* bookstore shelf. To most, it's a *religious* book, filled with religious words, written by religious people a long time ago. Definitely not "self-help."

At first glance, it seems they're right. A self-help book's table of contents lists chapters like "Practice the 3-P Plan" and "Disable the Disfunction Junction." Compare that to the Bible's table of contents: "Leviticus" and "Philemon" and "Lamentations"—somehow that doesn't look fun. The word Revelation looks promising . . . until you flip to that section and catch the part about a big red dragon with seven heads. And if that doesn't stop you, the giant prostitute will. It's enough to send any self-helper running to safer shelves.

Despite the unpromising table of contents, the dragons and the prostitutes, and all the other things that seem self-unhelpful, the Bible is rich in practical advice, and makes a bold claim on its efficacy in treating life's challenges. **Check out *2 Timothy 3:16–17*.**

Paul was a Bible expert—he knew the Old Testament blindfolded, and was pretty familiar with the new stuff too, being the author of much of it. If Paul says every bit is helpful, then it must be so. Still, some sections offer more *immediate* help than others. To find them, look for the popular teachers. For 2,000 years, the most popular teacher in the world has been Jesus. His lessons are simple, practical, and meant to be applied immediately. Let's hear some of his practical advice. **Read *Matthew 6:31–34*.**

This passage is not a commandment. It's not a harsh rebuke. It's just good advice, straight and simple. Here's how you can tell. First, it states the *problem*: worry. Then it tells you how to *solve* the problem: Put God first. Finally, it reveals the *benefits* of this advice: The stuff you've been worrying about will be taken care of for you.

I've heard, read, sung, and taught this simple passage at least a thousand times. So why don't I *do* it? It comes down to *control*. As a poor college student, I worried that I'd go to bed hungry. When I graduated, so did my worry; I fretted about undercooking my baked potatoes. Now I worry that the restaurant will get my dinner order wrong. And if I ever strike it rich, I'm sure I'll worry that the caterer will order the wrong brand of caviar for the dinner party.

I always manage to worry about what I can't control. No matter how much power I gain over my world, there's always a chunk or sliver I cannot master, and no matter how big or small that part is, it receives the full portion of my worry.

My problem isn't the circumstances. It's my *focus*. Jesus knows we can never be the absolute master of our world. That position is filled. So he offers us some inside information: Focus on the Master—he'll provide what all our worrying cannot.

PRACTICAL ADVISORS

The Gospels are filled with the Teacher's best advice. When he gives some, take notes. You're hearing them from the wisest Person in the universe. But his advice is not just wise, it's *practical*. He tested it on himself, in real-life situations, right here on this planet.

Jesus isn't the only practical teacher in the Bible. His kid brother James wrote his own self-help book packed with simple wisdom. **Take a look at *James 1:19–20*.**

Problem: speaking out in anger. Solution: shut up and listen. Benefit: a righteous life pleasing to God. You can pay a counselor hundreds of dollars to learn that bit of advice. You can pay a divorce lawyer thousands to help you remember it. Or you can take it as a free tip from Jesus' half brother.

The New International Version includes a tip within this tip. "My dear brothers, take note of this." Writing a note is not a bad idea. I need to put this note next to my phone, on every page of my appointment calendar, and write it on my hand whenever I go in public.

APPLY IMMEDIATELY

As you've probably figured out by now, I chose these three samples of biblical advice because they're the ones I most need to apply in my own life. As the good advisor James says, "Do not merely listen to the word, and so deceive yourselves. Do what it says" (1:22).

You can study the Bible's histories, marvel at its prophecies, ponder the poetry, stow away on the adventures, and compare the realities, all in an armchair. But the Bible's practical advice is only good if you apply it immediately. Don't store for future reference—by then it's too late. Like medicine, it won't work until you take it.

With advice passages, the enjoyment isn't in the reading; it's in the results. For best results, apply directly.

LESSON OF THE DAY

For best results, apply directly—
and keep applying till you see results.

PART TWO

How It's Organized

The Pentateuch

Savor the Good Parts

As a package, the first five books of the Old Testament are still called by their old Greek name. The "penta" is obvious to anyone who stayed awake in geometry class; "teuch" (rhymes with kook) means scroll, volume, or book. *Genesis* (origin, beginning), *Exodus* (going out) and *Deuteronomy* (second law) also come from the Greek. How did all these Hebrew writings end up with Greek names?

In the third century B.C., the Old Testament Scriptures were translated into that language in a collection that came to be called the *Septuagint*. That strange name comes from the Latin word for "seventy," based on the tradition that the king of Egypt hired 72 Palestinian Jews to transcribe it all in 70 days.

Now that we've had our language lesson for the day, let's get on with the story. Act 1, scene 1 opens with the lead character, God, making good things happen. (Hint: That's a recurring theme.) Then the other main characters enter the stage: first the humans, then Satan close on their heels. That's when the trouble starts, and it won't stop until some 1,200 pages later, when one of these characters makes a fiery exit. More on that later.

The first five books of the Bible tell the beginning of this epic story: God makes things perfect, Satan gets the first humans to mess it all up, and they and their descendants get scattered, drowned, kidnapped, enslaved, and dragged through the desert on their various adventures with and without God. The fifth book (Deuteronomy) ends about where the first one began: God's about to make good things happen again and his humans are going to get their second chance, in a land that's not as nice as the first one but a whole lot better than the last.

FIVE-BOOK TOUR

Taken as a whole, the five books of this section are referred to by Jesus and his contemporaries as the Law of Moses, for reasons that become painfully clear in the middle of Exodus. Moses is most likely its author; no one but an eyewitness could have recorded the details of his conversations with God—with few exceptions, an eyewitness of God is a dead witness. Moses also had intimate knowledge of Egyptian customs, language, and politics, which accounts for the details of such things in Exodus.

As for his account of everything that happened before his time, Moses undoubtedly had access to the rich oral history of the Jews, who had a knack for keeping track through thick and thin, as we saw last week. And considering the closeness of his relationship with God, it's safe to assume that he picked up some details straight from the Source. Deuteronomy records the author's own death—a tough trick for any author. Again, we assume that someone else picked up his pen at that point.

Let's take a quick look at each of Moses' famous books so you can find your way around on the next visit.

Genesis

Genesis is appropriately named, considering that it's the first book in the collection and that it describes the beginning of the universe. You can divide the book pretty cleanly into two parts right near the end of chapter 11. The first part deals with the Big events: Creation, the Fall, Noah and the Flood, and the scattering of the humans after the Babel Tower disaster. There's a lot going on here.

Things settle down a bit starting at chapter 12. The author introduces the key figures, or *patriarchs*, that got the Hebrew race started. The first person to be called a "Hebrew" is Abraham (14:13). Abraham's son is Isaac, his tribe-starting grandson is Jacob (who also goes by the name Israel), and his most notable great-grandson is Joseph. Of course he had lots of other descendants in those three generations, but the story stays close to these guys. In fact, Abraham, Jacob, and Joseph (but not Isaac) get at least ten chapters each. Over half the book of Genesis covers just these three men.

Joseph's story is told in the last 14 chapters of the book. His jealous brothers sell him into slavery. Joseph ends up in Egypt, gets a good job working for Pharaoh, and eventually reunites with his brothers and invites everyone, including their father, Jacob, to come live in Egypt. Genesis ends with the death of Joseph.

Exodus

Exodus is another excellent title because it covers the Jews' spectacular exit from the Egyptian stage. We'll be there in a moment. First, the story jumps a few hundred years from Joseph's death to Moses' birth. How times have changed. When Joseph died, the Jews were a single extended family of welcome guests in Egypt. Now they're an exploding nation of slaves. The pharaoh now in office launches an extreme form of population control, ordering all male infants to be thrown into the Nile. Moses' mom obeys the order . . . with but one minor adjustment: She sticks him in a basket first.

Pharaoh's daughter finds the floating tot, adopts him, and soon Moses is in tight with the royal family, just as his ancestor Joseph had been before him. As an adult, Moses makes a stupid career move when he kills an Egyptian caught abusing a Jew. He goes on the lam in Midian to avoid the murder rap. It's here that God introduces himself, by way of the famous flaming shrubbery. Moses returns to Egypt on a mission from God—to free the Jewish slaves and lead them to the Promised Land.

Pharaoh gives in to Moses' demands only through plaguey persuasion, then changes his mind just in time to get soaked in the Red Sea. And that's how the Israelites make it out of Egypt and begin what they hope to be a short trip through the desert.

Three months after their hasty Egyptian departure, the Jews camp out at the foot of Mount Sinai. This is where God makes the grand public appearance we looked at on the first day of our own journey. God signs a contract with the people, delivering the Ten Commandments and dozens of lesser laws to keep them safe and sane. God also gives them the blueprint for a portable tabernacle, as well as details for staffing and furnishing it.

After the unfortunate Golden Calf incident, in which the people manage to break most of the laws in one bacchanalian bash, God renews his contract, and Moses gets the folks started on the tabernacle project. Exodus ends with God's glory taking up residence in the brand-new tabernacle. It's easy to find in that giant tent-city: Just look for the cloud during the day, and fire at night.

Leviticus

Leviticus means "pertaining to the Levites." Levi was one of Jacob's twelve sons and Joseph's brother. God decreed that all priests should come from Levi's tribe; that is, his descendants. So it figures that this book is a manual for priests, telling how to conduct the various sacrifices and offerings and other religious duties assigned to them.

This manual fits well right after Exodus because the tabernacle has just been completed and now the priests need to know what to do with it. Leviticus explains their jobs. After the excitement of Exodus, Leviticus just seems to sit there—no heavenly fireworks, no miraculous water tricks—just rules and procedures. And in fact it does just sit there, because that's what the Israelites are doing at the moment. They don't continue their journey till the priest manual is complete.

But that doesn't mean it has to be boring. When you read Leviticus, you get the clear impression that God is not to be trifled with. He's very specific about his demands and expects them to be carried out to the letter. You also get an idea of how much disobedience hurts him. When he lays out the recipe for a sacrifice, you know that sin is expensive—to God *and* sinner. Reading the sin-by-sin payments of the Old Covenant give you a greater appreciation of Jesus' once-and-for-all sacrifice.

Through all the rules and regulations, you can see a God who's deeply concerned for his people. He has a nation to raise up and a Son to deliver through them—he doesn't want them dying from diseased foods, bad hygiene, or civil chaos. He's a strict yet loving parent who wants his kids to survive in their new world.

Numbers

Numbers is the English equivalent of *Arithmoi*, the Septuagint's title for this book. It got that name because it starts out with a math quiz. After delivering all the rules recorded in Exodus and Leviticus, God tells Moses to make a head count of all adult males in the camp at the foot of Mount Sinai. The final figure comes to 603,550 (1:46), which doesn't include women, children, or Levite men. As priests, the Levites weren't allowed to fight, so the number gives Moses a count of available soldiers. Throw in the civilians, and you get somewhere between two and three million Israelites. Big camp.

After celebrating their first annual Passover, they break camp and make a beeline for Kadesh-Barnea. God tells Moses to send out a dozen spies to sneak into the Promised Land to get an idea of what they're up against. They return with a mixed report: The good news is, it's a great place to live; the bad news is, the people already living there will tear them to shreds. After hearing the news, the people are ready to mutiny: "We should choose a leader and go back to Egypt" (14:4). Bad move.

God had tested their faith, and they failed miserably. What would have been a reasonably short trip to Canaan turns into a 40-year misadventure. The rest of the book tells what happened in the wilderness—pop quizzes and failures, rebellions and reprisals, encounters with the locals, a talking donkey, and Moses' own disobedience, which we discussed last week.

Numbers ends with the Israelites camped on the eastern side of the Jordan River, making plans for the conquest, division, and government of the Promised Land.

Deuteronomy

Deuteronomy isn't actually the "second law"; it's the same law set forth a second time. But it is a second *chance*. After wimping out at Kadesh-Barnea, the Israelites have had 39 more years to get their lives in order, their priorities straight, and their children in shape to do what the parents failed to do. The book of Numbers left them on the plains of Moab, just shy of the goal line. In Deuteronomy, Moses calls a time-out and gives his final messages to them.

His audience is too young to remember the Red Sea crossing; they missed out on God's big entrance at Mount Sinai and arrived too late in life to catch the first giving of the law. Moses gives them a history lesson. He recounts the episodes that brought the Israelites to this place and reviews the contract they have with God. He concludes his message with warnings and encouragement for each of the tribes.

Deuteronomy ends as Moses finishes his life's to-do list: Commission Joshua as the new leader, write the Law into a book (a book we now call the Pentateuch), go up the mountain and see the Promised Land in the distance, die. Moses completes the list.

THE GOOD PARTS

The recurring theme of the Pentateuch is clear: Obey God, life is good. Disobey God, life stinks. God himself repeats it page after page. Here's one of his first direct affirmations of this fact. **Read** *Exodus 15:26.*

Let's pause a moment: I'm assuming that you followed instructions last week and looked up the passages in your Bible. (If you didn't, you're a naughty reader, but I forgive you.) Now we've started a whole new part of this Bible-enjoyment plan, and taking visits to your Bible is even more important than before. We're on a sightseeing tour, after all, and it does no good just to sit on the bus. So step outside and into your Bible. Do it here and at all future tour stops. We'll wait till you snap a picture of the Exodus passage. But hurry—we've got a schedule to keep.

The consequences of sin are devastating. Obedience brings healing. This theme works as well now as it did in the beginning. What's more, it works for your reading. The best stories recount acts of obedience and the great things that resulted. The tedious parts (and the gory ones, too) tell of disobedience and the gruesome results. Of course, it's good to read *all* of it, but linger in the good stuff.

Savor the stories of faithfulness and the fruit they produce. Revel in the thrill of victory God shared with those who rallied to him. Bask in the warmth of the blessing God placed on those who turned to him. The same God who brought good things to his people back then is eager to bless you today.

LESSON OF THE DAY

*Savor the good parts; bask in the warmth
of God's blessings on the obedient.*

Historical Books:
Joshua to 2 Kings

Pay Attention

After the Israelites have spent forty years in a holding pattern out in the desert, God's about to do another good thing: give his people the clearance to land. The historical books chronicle their arrival. But in the spirit of their fickle ancestors, the new generations eventually turn a good thing into a bad thing. The blessings of obedience are forgotten; the Jews turn their back on God and pay the price. When they come to their senses, God does *another* good thing and restores them to himself.

HISTORY CONDENSED

The Old Testament's historical books cover a span of nearly 1000 years, from the crossing of the Jordan River around 1400 B.C. to Nehemiah's Jerusalem renewal project around 450 B.C. Most of this history is covered in the first seven books of the Historical section, which take us to the big Babylonian defeat in 586 B.C. Here's a condensed version.

Joshua

Joshua is named after its author, whom God chose to succeed Moses on the long meander to greener pastures. The book begins where the Pentateuch left us—on the east bank of the Jordan River. A former spy himself, Joshua sends two new spies over to Jericho on the west bank to see what they're up against on their first conquest. The spies are befriended and protected by a prostitute named Rahab.[1] The sneaky pair return to Joshua with their report. Joshua leads the people across the temporarily dry Jordan in a scene much like the Red Sea crossing. Joshua and his buddy Caleb are among the few old enough to appreciate the similarity: The rest of their generation died in the wilderness. And of the twelve original spies, only these two can claim this as a repeat visit.

High and dry on the west bank, Joshua leads the people to Jericho, taking the city with a shout. Only Rahab and her family are saved in the massacre. The rest of the book recounts the conquest and division of Canaan—who fought whom, and which tribes settled where. Like Deuteronomy, this book ends with the hero's death. The writer who finished Joshua's book for him gives the author a rare epitaph: Israel served God during the full length of this hero's leadership.

Judges

Judges is named for the military and civil leaders who ruled the Israelites in a loose confederacy before the monarchy was instituted. The author of the book is unknown. Unlike the last book, Judges is filled with examples of disobedience and its consequences. In defiance of God's clear instructions, the Jews allow some of the land's locals to remain, and problems spring up everywhere—wars, oppression, corruption, captivity. The delivering judges—Deborah, Gideon, Samson, and others—rescue the Jews from their predicaments and seek to set them on the right path.

God chooses unlikely heros in this book. Gideon is Mr. Milquetoast, demanding proof after proof that God has indeed called him to the rescue; when he finally complies, God entrusts him with just 300 men to fight an entire nation. Samson is Gideon's opposite—the Schwarzenegger of old, whose demise comes not in battle but from a bad-hair day.

The book of Judges covers 350 turbulent years and ends with its own condemning summary: "In those days Israel had no king; everyone did as he saw fit."

Ruth

Ruth is a refreshing sidebar to Judges, a story of love and faith and family among people who chose to serve God while surrounded by faithlessness. We don't know the name of the author; the book is named after its exceptional lead character. Ruth is a Moabite. When her husband dies, Ruth goes to Bethlehem to live with her Jewish mother-in-law Naomi. Ruth's faith catches the eye and eventually the heart of Boaz, a local man of the tribe of Judah. They get married and have a son, Obed.

Here's the best part. Obed has a kid named Jesse, and one of Jesse's sons becomes Israel's greatest king. In other words, King David's great-grandmother was a poor Gentile foreigner named Ruth. Many, many generations later another Son would be born from this same line, in this same town. And he would become the kinsman-redeemer of Jews *and* Gentiles.

1 Samuel

First Samuel is named after the key figure in the early chapters, who most likely wrote some of the book. Samuel was the last judge to reign after the period covered in Judges. From the start, you know Samuel is special. He's the miracle baby of a childless woman named Hannah. She makes a promise to God that if he grants her a child, she'll give it to him in thanks. God does his part, Hannah does hers, and Eli the priest gets to raise a son right, after getting it wrong with his own kids before.

Samuel shakes the Israelites to their spiritual senses and sends them on their knees to God. Unfortunately, in their revived national fervor they start clamoring for a king. "You've got a King," say Samuel and the Almighty. But they insist on the earthly variety, so Samuel appoints Saul—a sorry choice, as it turns out.

The book covers these and other events to occur in a century of Jewish history, including King Saul's escapades in evil, and the many adventures of David on his winding way to the throne. The book ends with Saul's death.

2 Samuel

Second Samuel continues the story without interruption, covering the next forty years of Israel's history. David mourns Saul's death, then takes the throne—which starts some very good things for friends of God and many unhappy endings for his enemies. The new king sets out to complete the work Joshua started, chasing out the entrenched locals. Things go great till David has a midlife crisis. He stays home from the war, has an affair with the wife of someone who didn't, and commits murder in an attempt to cover his adulterous tracks. Nathan is not fooled and slams David for his sins. The baby conceived in the affair dies, but Bathsheba—who's now David's wife—has another child; he figures big in the next book and more besides.

David's family troubles aren't over. "Like father, like son" is paid out in a double portion: David's son Amnon rapes his own half-sister; another son, Absalom, avenges his sister by killing their rapist brother. Absalom escapes for a few years, then returns as mutineer, leading the people to war against his own father. The rebel son eventually gets caught and killed in a riding accident involving an oak tree (an arboreal altercation often reenacted in Western films). David restores his reign, but it's not as much fun as it used to be.

In a fit of independence and against wise counsel, David orders a count of available soldiers—apparently to reassure himself of his battle strength. But the God who led Joshua to victory with a shout and gave Gideon just 300 men to take a nation isn't pleased when David puts might ahead of righteousness, and the nation is hit with a three-day plague in consequence. David grabs the message and gets right with God.

1 Kings

First Kings rolls the royal story through another century or so. David is now an old man; his last duty is to appoint the new king. His son Adonijah is champing at the bit, but Dad makes it clear that Bathsheba's son Solomon will be the new man in charge. David dies, and the young Solomon ascends to the throne. Solomon is known for many great works, but he slept through his greatest. In a dream, the young king asks God for understanding. The Lord is so pleased, he grants the request . . . and throws in wealth and honor besides.

Solomon invests his gifts immediately to establish a solid government, profitable relationships with foreign countries, and a permanent temple in downtown Jerusalem. Solomon also invests in exotic women, accepting an army of foreign wives through his far-flung international alliances. His household becomes a Hall of Wacky Religions, each wife mixing her own brand of incense and idolatry down the street from the One True God Temple.

On Solomon's death, his son Rehoboam ascends to the throne. Disregarding his father's advisors, the new king vows to raise taxes. The ten northern tribes secede from the union and make Jeroboam their king. Rehoboam is left with the territories of Judah and Benjamin in the south, the former becoming the name of the new state. The divorce takes place in chapter 12, leaving us to pay alternating visits to each of the former partners as it descends through a line of kings, most of them awful. In the contest of who can descend further, Israel wins, but Judah is close behind. God is still in the picture, revealing himself through Elijah in the north, and in the south through the good deeds of rare kings like Asa and Jehoshaphat.

2 Kings

Second Kings continues the two nations' decline into disobedience, depravity, and captivity. Like the previous book, it jumps back and forth, telling the sorry deeds of each nation's current king. Israel's royal line is consistently rotten, which leads them into enslavement with the Assyrians. Judah manages to hold out longer, thanks in part to an occasional godly king, but they eventually follow the fate of their northern kin when the Babylonians come to town.

Elijah is clearly God's favorite hero in 1 Kings. In 2 Kings, the title goes to his protégé, Elisha. He pulls a Solomonesque prayer stunt by asking God for a double-portion of the Spirit that propelled Elijah, and gets it. Elisha's godly adventures are especially refreshing in a book brimming with the accounts of Israel's godless leaders.

Judah survives over a century after Israel is taken, yet the book gives it less coverage—partly because its several good kings tended to reign longer, giving the writers less dirt to shovel. That leaves Judah to act out the last chapters alone, and they don't do so well. Check out the beginning of the end: **Read 2 Kings 24:8–14.**

Soon after this moment, the Babylonian army returns to finish the job. Judah's citizens are hauled off to Babylon and the temple is destroyed. The Jews are back where they started: on the wrong side of the Jordan, ready to try again.

IT PAYS TO PAY ATTENTION

The Israelites' on-again, off-again relationship with God is painful to watch. It's easy to spot their wrong turns because we can see their past clearly and know what's ahead. To us, decades and even centuries fly by with the turn of a page. But the Israelites had to live it all in *real* time, day by day, year after year. Their recollections of great moments faded quickly, pushed out by the urgencies of the here and now. From their vantage point, what happened to their fathers and grandfathers was ancient history.

We can relate. How many of us can recall all the lessons of our own past, much less those of our parents and grandparents? Life moves *fast*. It's all we can do just to keep up. The great spiritual events of our own lives don't stick in our hearts and minds quite as long as we thought they would. Memories, even the best ones, fade.

The trick is to keep paying attention. Despite how it may look to us, the Jews didn't wake up one morning and say, "The past was great, but today let's try something completely new." It was more subtle than that. They woke up each morning with a little less enthusiasm, allowed the important lessons of the past to die slowly in their memories, and little by little, generation to generation, lost their way.

We can learn a lot from their missteps. Regular sessions with God recall to us great spiritual moments in our past and prepare us for the big moments ahead. It's hard to lose your way when you keep your eyes on the Leader.

And that's a good way to read these historical books. Pay attention and keep your eye on the Leader. When the Jews wander off track, recall a moment in your own life when you did the same. Ask, *What are they forgetting? What did I forget that took me down my wrong turn?* Then spot what it is that brought them around. See if the same thing hasn't happened to you.

Most important, check in with God as often as you can. He'll help you remember the great moments in the journey so far, and show you the good stuff ahead.

LESSON OF THE DAY

Pay attention; follow God closely. . . . He's the only One who knows the right path.

Historical Books:
1 Chronicles to Esther

Marvel At Works of Restoration

As I pointed out in yesterday's lesson, the first batch of history books begins and ends on the wrong side of the Jordan River. In each case, God's people are there as a consequence of their own sin. Like most people, the Jews had a pernicious tendency to repeat the errors of their past. They replayed the same song with mind-numbing regularity. Here's the chorus: Take God's blessing, mess it up, pay the price, wise up, crawl back to God. Repeat chorus.

What's amazing is that God continued to listen to their song. Whenever they came crawling back, he picked them up, dusted them off, and gave them a clean start. And he did so with his whole heart. The blessings he bestowed on Joshua, David, Solomon, Ruth, Elijah, and many faithful others were not cheap baubles from a jilted lover; they were love gifts from a God ever eager to start afresh.

REPRISE

The historical books from 1 Chronicles to Esther tell the story of God giving the Jews another chance. The two Chronicles take us back to the beginning, to retell the history that got them where they are. Ezra, Nehemiah, and Esther carry us into new and better years. After all the bad news in the previous books, it's a welcome change.

1 Chronicles

First Chronicles is a flashback to the key events covered in the earlier history books. The previous book, 2 Kings, ends with Israel working for the Assyrians, Judah on forced assignment elsewhere. And so they will remain until we get through the Chronicles. Traditionally, Ezra has been considered the author. Like his predecessor Moses, Ezra was keen on giving the long-captive Jews a sense of where they came from and what they were about. The Chronicles are his history lesson.

It's a short course: In the first book he gets us from Adam to Solomon in just 29 short chapters. That takes some serious editing. In the first nine chapters the writer cuts out most of the stories and sticks with the genealogy. David makes his entrance in chapter 10; his story comprises the rest of the book. Ezra is much kinder to David than the writer of 2 Samuel. He leaves out the Bathsheba incident, the royal incest, and other sins, although he does cover the disastrous census.

It's clear that the Chronicles are not written as an account of what went wrong in their past but as a foundation for rebuilding what was *right*. The writer is providing the reformed nation with a blueprint for political and religious life, calling the new generation to order and obedience in what works best.

2 Chronicles

Second Chronicles is the second semester of Ezra's history course—presented in the same style and with the same purpose as the first installment. The text begins with Solomon and ends with Judah in exile. But unlike 1 and 2 Kings, 2 Chronicles limits itself to Judah alone, which makes sense, considering the author's heritage and scope of knowledge.

Solomon, the builder of God's temple, figures big in the first nine chapters, giving us a hint of what Ezra would like to see happen when his students get resettled in their homeland. In the remainder of the book, the author covers the subsequent kings, going light on their sins and heavy on their successes.

The book concludes with the best news we've heard in a century. I'll let you listen to it yourself: **Read 2 Chronicles 36:23.**

That's quite a proclamation. Cyrus, the king of Persia (and now king of the conquered Babylonians) grants the Jews permission to return to Jerusalem to rebuild their Father's house.

Ezra

Ezra is named after its main character and probable author. After his fast-moving history course, the professor now leaps into current events: getting back to Jerusalem to rebuild a temple, a faith, and a nation. Call it a revival course.

When King Cyrus announces the welcome-home decree, Zerubbabel, the grandson of one of Judah's last wicked kings, leads about 50,000 Jews back to their homeland to get started on the temple reconstruction effort. After the foundation is laid, the project gets mixed reviews: The young folks are thrilled; the old folks, who remember the grandeur of Solomon's version in the good old days, weep in disappointment.

Political bickering puts the project on hold for several years until Darius, the new king in Persia, renews the promise of his predecessor. And just to be sure it is carried out, he funnels taxes into the endeavor. The temple is completed.

A half century later, Ezra—who's still in exile, by the way—gets his chance to return to the homeland. Within months of his arrival, he shakes the city into revival, recalling the people to their covenant with God. For the Jews, things are looking up again.

Nehemiah

Nehemiah is named for its author, the cupbearer to the Persian king Artexerxes. While in the king's employ, Nehemiah hears news of the sad state of Jerusalem's defenses—the walls are broken, the gates are burned. After praying to God about the situation, he approaches his boss and asks for permission to go to the troubled city to put things in order. The king grants his request.

Within days of his arrival, this godly building contractor inspects the site, recruits a labor force, and gets the project rolling. Nehemiah cuts through a mountain of red tape and criticism to finish the project in 52 days. At the dedication ceremony, Nehemiah and Ezra stand side by side and invite the people to celebrate God's blessing. Soon afterward, Nehemiah takes off his hard hat and puts on his governor's uniform, restoring the social and religious practices that had once made their nation strong. He must have taken Ezra's history course—by the end of his term, Judah is thriving in God's ways.

Esther

Esther is out of sequence; it covers events back in Persia before Ezra returns to Jerusalem. We don't know who wrote it. The book is named for the Jewish queen of the Persian king Xerxes. Esther gets that plush job after cousin Mordecai enters her in the king's personal beauty pageant. Esther takes first place, which means she gets to marry the king (and wear the best beauty pageant crown ever).

When Mordecai gets wind of a plot to kill all the Jews in Persia, he sends a message to his cousin so she can use her influence to stop it. Esther initially dismisses the message ... until Mordecai replies with a warning that her sweet position won't save her from genocide. (The former Mrs. Xerxes lost her title simply by refusing to come when called.) Then he adds a subtle reminder of Who she works for: "Who knows but that you have come to royal position for such a time as this?" (4:14).

Esther petitions her husband, who stamps out the plot and plotters. Then Esther and Mordecai work together to do more good things for the Jews.

The book is unique among the histories because not once does it mention God. But if you read between the lines, you find him on every page. God's preservation of the Jews, even in captivity, restores them to prayer and fasting and hopeful obedience.

RESTORATION IN PROGRESS

Let's face it, if God were not able to restore us to himself, with his heart on our future and no mind for the past, he'd have walked off the stage long ago. But from first to last, he hangs in there. Time and time again, he proves that his love can outlast our apathy, any day in the week, any period in history.

He's the ultimate reunion planner, the wise counselor of reconciliation, the master restorer. With few exceptions, the tumbled-down moments in this Jewish history are rebuilt with the turn of a page. As you read the historical books, watch for the Restorer in action. Again and again, you'll catch God in the act of rebuilding walls, temples, cities, nations . . . and people.

On your next visit to this section, breeze past the unpronounceable names. Don't trouble yourself with royal dynasties or smudgy wall-builder's blueprints. Instead, marvel at God's restoration works. Contemplate the depth of a love that will go to these extremes to recover what was lost. Then let him go to work on restoring you.

Marvel at works of restoration—in the Bible, in the lives around you, in God's great act of restoring you to himself.

Poetical Books

Read Out Loud

The writers of the poetical books grappled with life's intangibles, crafting words and phrases to form answers to our deepest questions: What is God's character? How can we know him? How can we please him? What does he think of us? Why does he allow evil? What is the meaning of life? What is love?

Questions like these are simple to ask, difficult to answer. Our libraries overflow with works from those who've tried. Their attempts tend to fall into two categories: philosophical treatises that devolve into brain-straining labyrinths of logic and conjecture, or flowery feel-good journeys to nowhere. Then there's the work of the Bible's poets.

THE COLLECTION

The historical books focus on the past; the prophetical books have their eye on the future.

Stuck between them are the poetical books, which focus on the ever-present here and now.[1] While all the books grapple with life's big questions, each reveals the answers in a unique style.

Job

Job is a mysterious book—we don't know who wrote it or when it was recorded. Its title character probably lived in the time of Abraham. While its origin may be a mystery, its theme is crystal clear: Why does a God of love and mercy allow bad things to happen to good people? The book of Job explores the answer.

Job is a wealthy, popular, faithful man of God—the perfect test subject. God allows Satan to inflict compounding tragedies on Job to see how he fares when his blessings run out. When the Enemy is through, Job has lost his kids, crops, livestock—everything but his (nagging) wife. Now he's got nothing left to do but scrape his boils and argue with his friends.

Each friend attempts to identify the cause and solution to Job's trouble. In the end it's God himself, speaking from a whirlwind, who argues best. For the answer, you'll have to read the transcript yourself: You'll find it in chapters 38 through 41.

Psalms

Psalms is a hymn book—a collection of songs compiled by the ancient Jews. David wrote half of them (remember, he made his royal debut as King Saul's harpist). His son Sol wrote a pair, and various other songwriters, including Moses, composed the rest.

Compared to modern hymn writers, the psalmists were a pretty free-spirited bunch. They didn't limit themselves to praise and worship songs. In fact, they wrote songs that tell history, prophecy, conquest, corruption, regret. They even threw in some inflammatory jingles against their enemies: Imagine singing Psalm 58 at *your* next church service: "Oh God, shatter their teeth in their mouth. . . ."

When reading the psalms, it's helpful to remember who heard them first. The ancient Jews had no printing press, so the only people who could actually read the Scriptures were the priests and scribes—the religious elite—who had access to the original writings or the precious few copies. As we discussed on Day 4, the common folk didn't *read* God's Word, they *heard* it. And as any advertiser will attest, the best way to get people to remember your message is to set it to music. Then repeat it as often as possible.

The psalm writers set God's Word to music, to be sung again and again. Apparently, the *tunes* themselves weren't so important; they were merely the vehicles used to carry the message to the people. That's a good thing, because we don't have a record of those notes. What's better, their absence gives us creative license to set the words to our own choice of music—classical, jazz, rock, rap, country, polka—or any other genre, in any culture, at any period. Future generations will undoubtedly invent new styles of music and sing the psalms' timeless words to sounds as yet unheard.

So if what you're actually reading is a song, try singing it. If you've experienced a lot of praise and worship music, you'll hear some of the popular psalms in your head. For other songs, try reading them as you listen to instrumental music—pick the style to match your taste and the mood of the psalm. With a little experimenting, you'll find that the words dance on the music . . . while your heart moves to their message.

Proverbs

Proverbs is Solomon's treatise on wisdom, with a few contributions from Agur and Lemuel, two wiseguys we know nothing about. Of Solomon we know plenty. He was asleep when he acquired his wisdom but wide awake when he wrote a book about it. Sol's insight presents a delightful paradox: God is the pinnacle, inventor, and provider of all wisdom, so it seems wisdom is not an easy thing to attain, yet most of the book delivers bonehead simple, immediately attainable, intensely practical steps toward wisdom. Doesn't that seem like a contradiction?

That's the beauty of Proverbs. In it we learn that God's wisdom is not about facts and figures; the Almighty is not a dusty-handed professor standing before a chalkboard, diagraming obtuse forces and formulae that govern the ways of the world. The Omniscient One is the author of life itself, eager to share the secrets to successful living, in simple terms we humans can understand. Does he share all this wisdom in just one book? Of course not. But he tells us where to look for the rest: in *himself*.

In that sense, Proverbs is like a sampler—a collection of tips for practical living that whets our appetite for more. To satisfy that appetite, we must go straight to the Source. Through prayer, obedience, reflection, and wise counsel from others who are connected to the Source, we can download much more.

So when you read the advice in this book, consider the Source. These are not just suggestions or opinions or quaint ancient sayings. They're small bites of wisdom from the One who knows everything. When you've digested a morsel, ask for another helping.

Ecclesiastes

Ecclesiastes is a Greek word meaning "preacher." The author of this book refers to himself as "the Preacher, son of David, king in Jerusalem"—a rather long pen name for a guy named Sol. The book reads like a sermon transcript. The preacher just happens to be the richest, wisest, most powerful person in Israel, so he speaks with authority when he says that all earthly pursuits turn up empty without God.

Like most good sermons, Ecclesiastes uses a series of illustrations to build a clear, solid message. Solomon juxtaposes the futility of various popular pursuits with the clear and unwavering purpose of God in and for our lives.

Solomon certainly wasn't the last guy to deliver this kind of testimonial. We've heard many a celebrity tell how he or she forsook the pointless pursuits of the flesh to find God. Unfortunately, many such stories leave us cold because they seem more about the delivered than the Deliverer. Solomon's message keeps God on top. And though most of us cannot relate to Solomon in his wealth and wisdom, we can still identify ourselves with the preacher because we've each felt that deep emptiness that comes from pursuing our own earthly treasures.

Ecclesiastes may be an ancient sermon, but it still rings true. We confirm this old preacher's conclusions in our own experiences daily. Here's a tip: Instead of just reading Ecclesiastes, preach it—aloud, to yourself. Let its timeless words ring in your ears.

Song of Songs

Song of Songs is Solomon's romantic poem, telling of the courtship and marriage to one of his many wives. It's rich in simile and metaphor, love and commitment, sexual attraction and emotional intimacy.

It seems strange that this book made it into the Bible. There's nothing wrong with the content; it's the author that gives us pause. If Solomon granted each of his women "equal time," it would have taken him the better part of three years to sleep through the roster. What business does *he* have telling us about marriage and commitment?

Then again, maybe that's what gives this poem its punch. Solomon surely must have known cynicism in love, the delay-fuse pain of detachment, the chill of evaporating ardor. Had he chosen to write about love's darker side, we'd certainly be reading a longer poem . . . and hearing more Bible verses in country music. But Sol, with wisdom and unparalleled perspective, writes of a committed love that even he can grow. There's hope for us after all.

BREAK THE SILENCE

Life's big questions often go unanswered because we're afraid to voice them. Secure in God's sovereignty, the writers of the poetical books spoke up. They asked tough questions and received answers from the One who knows best. We can follow their example by asking the same God the same questions.

You'll find many of his answers in this section of the Scripture. Read them aloud. Let's try that now. **Read (aloud)** *Ecclesiastes 3:1–8.*

This passage reads so well aloud that it's almost a crime to read it silently. (If you committed that crime just now, redeem yourself by rereading it audibly ... or sing it if you remember the popular version.) In a handful of verses, the poet describes the seasons of life we all know intimately well. He describes the world beyond our experience, too: He starts with "a time to be born" just as God bore the earth in the beginning, and ends with "a time for peace," which is what God promises his children for eternity. Death doesn't get the last line.

When you ponder life's big questions, search the poetical section. And when you find an answer, read it aloud. Some answers sound like whispers. Others weave themselves into song. And a few are best carried in a shout. You don't need punctuation or music notation to tell you how to read. Just play it by ear.

LESSON OF THE DAY

Read out loud—listen to God whisper,
sing, and shout the answers
to life's big questions.

Prophetical Books:
The Majors

Listen for God's Call

The word *prophecy* can be confusing. There are prophecies about the *future*, which is a pretty keen trick and explains why prophets who can do it get all the publicity. But there are also prophecies about *today's* truth: Prophets with this gift see the present, but their view is much clearer.

The Bible's prophetical books contain both kinds of prophecies: truth about the future, and truth for today. Each kind of prophecy served its purpose. Let's look first at a fore-telling prophecy: **Isaiah 9:6.**

That bit of information didn't do Isaiah's contemporaries a lot of good. What use could they make of it? But like a grower who plants a seed for a fruit tree that his grandson will first pick, Isaiah planted truth for the benefit of future generations. Let's fast-forward 700 years or so and take a look at the fruit: **Read John 3:16–17.**

A son was promised, and a son was delivered. These two short passages proved to later generations that God was still sitting at the controls. What's more, they alerted folks to other things said by those old-timers. "Gee, if he was right about that fact, maybe we ought to take a closer look at what else he said!"

But let's not forget those in-your-face, "tell it like it is" prophets. They had an often thankless and occasionally hazardous job. Prophets of the Lord were given an unenviable assignment: Tell the truth. People *say* they want the truth, but the truth they want to hear is the truth about others. Few of us are eager to hear the truth about ourselves. Pashhur the priest wasn't. God sent Jeremiah to the temple to lay down the facts about Judah's sins and their consequences. Being chief priest and all, Pashhur took it personally: **Check out** his reaction in *Jeremiah 20:1–3*.

Imagine what was going through Jeremiah's mind when he woke up that morning, knowing he was going to break the awful news to Pashhur and his pompous peers. Maybe he was thinking, *This is going to be fun. Can't wait to see the old guy squirm!* Or maybe he was dreading every moment, knowing that arrogant leaders have a violent reaction to criticism. We don't know what Jeremiah was thinking that morning, but we do know this: God sent him to deliver a message, and he did it.

MAJOR PROPHET ROSTER

It's important to note that each of the Old Testament prophets was called by God himself. The job wasn't a career choice but a divine appointment. The total roster of these appointments is greater than the number of prophetical books because prophets such as Elijah, Elisha, and Nathan, whose stories are told in the historical books, don't have their own books here.

The prophetical books come from prophets who lived immediately before, during and after Israel's and Judah's exiles—

roughly 750 to 400 B.C. These were rough times for the Jews, and most of the writings show it.

There are seventeen books in all, bunched into two groups: The first five are known as the "major prophets"; the rest are "minor prophets." The description is one of size, not stature. The major prophets just had more to say, but all spoke the truth and nothing but the truth. Here are the majors.

Isaiah

Isaiah lived in Judah around the time its northern neighbor Israel was being sacked by the Assyrians. Judah's kings are busy flirting with the same disaster. Isaiah's prophetic advice leads Judah to more prudent politics, but only through God's direct intervention are they saved from Israel's fate. Isaiah also spoke up about the Messiah quite a bit, but few understood who he was really talking about till Jesus himself fulfilled these prophecies.

Jeremiah

Jeremiah whipped out his words in Judah just before they were clobbered by the Babylonians. Jeremiah predicts Judah's impending doom, which doesn't go over big with the bureaucrats—they slap him with fists and restraining orders. At one point he has to send his secretary, Baruch, to proclaim the bad news in his place. When Judah falls, Jeremiah is abducted to Egypt, where he finishes out his prophecies and his days.

Lamentations

Lamentations is traditionally ascribed to Jeremiah, though he didn't sign his work. It's a collection of five poems in which the author laments the destruction of Jerusalem and the temple. The first four poems are acrostics, which we talked about earlier in this book. Their construction creates a doleful rhythm, like a funeral dirge, which is how the Jews still read it in their annual observance of the event Jeremiah laments. He had predicted this sad outcome for years, so it seems that he above all others would be most prepared for it. Yet when it comes to pass, he is heartbroken.

Ezekiel

Ezekiel is a contemporary of Jeremiah. He warns Judah of impending doom, and when that comes to pass, he's hauled off to Babylon. There he continues his prophecies, reminding the Jews in exile of the sin that put them there, and plants hope that they will one day be restored to God and homeland. In later chapters he leaps to the distant future, foretelling events to occur in Christ's second coming.

Daniel

Daniel also witnesses the fall of Jerusalem but doesn't begin prophesying till he lands a job in King Nebuchadnezzar's court. God speaks to him in dreams, which fascinate the king—and confound modern historians who can't understand how this young Jew could have described Greek and Roman conquests centuries before they happened. Daniel also predicts events in our own future. Based on his record, we can count on the truth of these too. The book also tells of Daniel's adventures in civil disobedience, which start with a menu dispute and end with some lions going to bed hungry.

THE PROBLEM WITH PROPHETS

Time for another confession: I don't really *enjoy* reading all the books I've just described! I get tired of hearing about the sins of Israel and Judah. Most of the time I already know *what's* going to happen with these predictions because they already *did* happen. Doesn't matter that they wrote in future tense—it's past tense to *me*. And for all the prophecies yet unfulfilled, I have no comprehension. Talk of the Tribulation's times and events loses me entirely.

I mean no disrespect when I confess these things—to God, to his prophets, or to those who enjoy reading these books. If you revel in prophetic revelation and are fascinated by discussions on the end times, these books are islands of treasure, destined to provide you with a lifetime of fruitful exploration. But I think you're exceptional; most of us struggle and trudge our way through this chunk of scriptures. What can we do to ease the journey?

The prophets say the same things over and over. Nag, nag, nag. Seldom does the audience listen. Ironically, they're still repeating themselves today—you can hear their voices by opening to their words. Is their *current* audience (that's us) listening? As most of us learned in childhood, the nagging generally stops only when we *do as we're told.* God is still using these prophets to call us to obedience. And he'll keep on calling till we do as we're told. When you read the prophets, replace Israel and Judah and other Jewish names with your own. Is the verse still true? Then you know what to do. If you don't heed the warning, the Enemy will surely attack.

Another problem is the confusion of names: The prophets use different monikers for the same thing, and the same name for different things. *Israel* refers to all Jews, except when it's just *Samaria*, which is also called *Ephraim*. The Chaldeans are from Babylon, but Babylonia is now Persian. It's hard to listen in on a conversation when you don't know who they're talking about. The best solution is to read the historical books first. Those writers give us a background of who's who ... and when and where they got their names. Another great help may be in the back of your Bible: a good map will show you the big names in the neighborhood. And if you have a study Bible, you might find the translated names in the margins.

The biggest challenge is making sense of the unfulfilled prophecies—the Tribulation, Christ's second coming, the millennial kingdom. If these prophecies confuse you, welcome to the club. Christians have been arguing these subjects since the church's opening day. To better understand these prophecies, it helps to read Revelation first. But not right now; we'll take a visit there in a few days.

GOD'S CALL

With few exceptions, the prophets relayed messages with little support from the heavenly audio-visual department. They just spoke them. And if the recipients weren't listening, God's message flew right over their heads. Maybe they were expecting a miraculous sign. Instead, they got plain words from someone straight off the street.

How about you? How does God call you? If you're waiting for a miraculous sign, you may be missing the message. Look around and listen up, because he may be speaking to you through more conventional means: a sermon, a sobering word from a friend, a haunting question from a spouse or child . . . and through the prophets themselves. These old guys may look a little strange and sound even stranger, but they're delivering God's message, so they're worth a listen. When you read the prophetical books, remember that they were God's urgent call to his people. Then ask yourself, "What message is God sending *me*?"

LESSON OF THE DAY

Listen for God's call—he's speaking through the Word and through his people. Don't miss his message.

Prophetical Books: The Minors

Deliver the Message

In yesterday's lesson, we saw God using the major prophets to deliver major messages to his people. The minor prophets deliver the same loud message; they just use fewer words. The majors read like long letters. The minors are more like telegrams.

The 12 books of the minor prophets fall into two subsections: The first nine prophets lived in the days preceding the Babylonian exile in 585 b.c. The last three in the collection are written by prophets after Judah's return to the homeland. They are the most recent books in the Old Testament. Here's a quick rundown.

Hosea

Hosea is a prophet for pre-exile Israel, a nation whose marriage to God looks a lot like Hosea's own marriage to Gomer. Hosea warns Israel of their sin and predicts the result.

Joel

Joel is Judah's earliest prophet and a specialist in the future. His big theme is the day of the Lord; he describes what will happen before, during, and after Christ's return in the last days of this world.

Amos

Amos is a sheep breeder from Judah who goes up to Israel to condemn their corruption. After a predictably hostile reception, he returns home to commit his words to writing.

Obadiah

This particular Obadiah (there are many others in the Old Testament) predicts his nation's doom as a result of their rejoicing over the trouble in neighboring Jerusalem.

Jonah

Jonah is alone among the prophets in his refusal to answer God's call—a choice he soon regrets. When God tells him to leave Israel and preach to the Assyrians in Ninevah, Jonah opts for a vacation in Spain instead. En route, he winds up on the wrong side of a fish, which regurgitates him only after he repents. This time he goes where he's told.

Micah

Micah preaches to the common people of Judah while his contemporary Isaiah is shaking up things at the palace. He cries out for social justice and predicts the birthplace of the Savior (see Matthew 2:3–6).

Nahum

Nahum, a prophet in Judah, gives the follow-up report on Jonah's revival efforts in Ninevah. The Assyrians there had failed to pass on the faith to their children, who grew up to stomp out Israel and have now begun kicking at Judah. Nahum predicts what's next for Ninevah: destruction.

Habakkuk

Habakkuk is a prophet of Judah in the dark days preceding the Babylonian invasion. He asks two tough questions: Why does God allow Judah's evil to go unpunished? How can God use people even more wicked than Judah to punish them? Habakkuk's answers predict Judah's fate—and give Paul and the author of Hebrews some of their best material.

Zephaniah

Zephaniah preaches to Judah during the good old days of King Josiah. But God shows him the future, and it's not pretty for Judah or its neighbors. He closes his tiny book with a vision of the glorious future of Christ's ultimate reign.

Haggai

Haggai is the first of the three books at the end of the prophetical section written by prophets after Judah's Babylonian exile. Haggai reprimands the people for stalling on the temple reconstruction project and encourages foreman Zerubbabel in the effort.

Zechariah

Zechariah echoes his contemporary Haggai in the call to finish the temple. Zechariah also has visions of the future—Christ's arrival the first time and what happens when he comes again.

Malachi

Malachi is the last voice heard in the Old Testament. A century has passed since the temple was completed, and the Jews have again lost the fervor stirred up by Zerubbabel and Nehemiah, Zechariah and Haggai. The last prophet rebukes the people for their lackluster faith, calls them to repentance, then finishes his book (and our Old Testament) with a curious prophecy: **Read *Malachi 4:5–6*.**

Malachi brings up an old prophet to prepare us for a new one. As it turns out, he's talking about John the Baptist (see Matthew 17:10–13). This new Elijah makes his appearance four silent centuries later—which comes just a few pages later in the Christian Bible.

DELIVER THE MESSAGE

When God sends a message, he expects it to be delivered (just ask Jonah). As the New Testament makes clear, it's not enough to *receive* the message; you've got to pass it on. You're holding a message in your heart, and the Lord wants you to deliver it to those around you. It reads like this: *Urgent message from God— "I love you. I sent my Son to die for you. I want to live with you now, then have you come live with me later. Please call."* That's a pretty important message. Who are you supposed to deliver it to?

Read the prophetical books as if you're listening in on God's phone call to his people. Then stay on the line and listen for his message to *you*. Listen carefully because he may be telling you to repeat the message.

LESSON OF THE DAY

Deliver the message—transmit God's urgent message to those around you.

The Gospels and Acts

See God with a Belly Button

In the Old Testament, God is the relentless lover of a fickle people. The New Testament opens with this Lover's most outrageous act: a personal appearance. The four Gospels recount the best and worst moments of his visit. Let's cut to his entrance.

I don't mean to sound snooty when I say this, but I think his entrance was ... well, unimpressive. On Mount Sinai he arrives with lightning, thunder, and an earthquake. In the desert he throws out a pillar of fire as a beacon. When Elijah has his day with the Baal cadets, God lets loose the pyrotechnics. This is impressive stuff.

Then in the New Testament, Jesus shows up. No fireworks, no earth shaking, not a single lightning bolt. Just a baby. A naked, bloody, crying, drooling, helpless infant. Born in a barn. Even had a belly button.

What's so special about *that*? Such arrivals occur every day. Sure, it's a big thing for the family and friends, but the world doesn't stop in its tracks to take notice. It takes a Superbowl to do that.

Well, I think I've figured out why God chose this unspectacular arrival route. He wasn't trying to impress us, amaze us, or scare us into attention. He was trying to tell us something: "I love you." Fireworks and natural disasters don't convey that message. It's the kind of message that's best delivered face-to-face. So God became a real human—with a real face we could look at (without melting), a real mouth to proclaim the message, and real hands and blood to prove its truth.

FOUR VIEWS AND AN EPILOGUE

The Gospels tell the story of God with a belly button, delivering his most important message. The book of Acts tells us what people did immediately after his visit. Here's how each of the books conveys the gospel story.

Matthew

Matthew picks up where Malachi left off. The Messiah has come, and Matthew meets him face-to-face. All the taxes that this collector might pocket could not fill the emptiness in his life. Matthew hears Jesus say, "Follow me" and leaves it all behind.

Every Jew knew his family tree—the tribe, clan, and homeland that defined his heritage. And thanks to the hints of the prophets, all knew the pedigree of the promised Messiah: tribe of Judah, line of David, to be born in the town of Bethlehem. To convince his Jewish readers that Jesus is indeed that Messiah, Matthew opens his Gospel with Jesus' genealogy, as credentials to those who knew a thing or two about the prophecies.

Jesus passes the heritage requirements but fails to live up to the religious leaders' other expectations. For one thing, they were looking for a sharp prophet like Elijah—good and godly with a few miracles thrown in to jazz things up. They weren't expecting God *himself*. For another, they were hoping for a Messiah who would toe the line, agree with their own teachings—a team player. Instead, they got Jesus—quick to contradict their message, confound their knowledge, and even criticize their hypocrisy.

Most of all, the Jews were eager for a Messiah who would kick the Romans out of town so they could have their own king, just like in the good old days of David. But when Jesus spoke of a kingdom, he was talking about God's, not theirs. Major disappointment.

Matthew knew their mistaken Messiah ideas and takes great pains to show that Jesus is in fact the real Messiah. Buried just beneath his words is a plea: "Forget what you thought you knew. Look again. With the eyes of a child, see the Messiah: the only hope for recovery, not for those who think they're healthy but for those who know they're sick." To the intractable leadership, the plea goes unheard. But to many others it meant the end of spiritual bondage: The King has freed us from the Great Oppressor.

Mark

Mark tells the same great story to a whole new crowd. In later books we learn that he's a missionary with his cousin Barnabas and their pal Paul, traveling around the Roman world to spread the Good News. Mark's Roman-world audience isn't expecting a Messiah; they don't much care about the king thing—they've got a Caesar on the throne. Unlike the Jews, who are engrossed in doctrine, theology, and family trees, the Romans revel in action, adventure, *results*. That's what Mark gives them.

He writes his Gospel so common folk can understand who Jesus is and why that's good news. Mark leaves out the genealogy, angelic birth announcement, and the baby showers, and jumps straight into the action: meet John the Baptist, confound Satan in the wilderness, recruit some working-class disciples. He touches but lightly on Jesus' confrontations with the religious elite, of whom his readers know little and care less. He uses just half the number of Old Testament references as Matthew—enough to show Jesus is a man with a past, but not enough to intimidate students of a different history.

Mark often avoids the stories of other people to keep Jesus in the spotlight. The result is a short, fast narrative that reads like the script to an action film. Only this Hero isn't busting heads and breaking hearts—he's miraculously healing the sick, performing more miracles, comforting the poor, feeding the hungry through miracles, and giving everyone a glimpse of a miraculous God on the move.

In case you didn't catch it, Mark is the book of miracles, miracles, and more miracles, performed by a servant named Jesus, who's the best thing ever to happen to humans. There's no better call than to serve him, but if you do, you'd better keep on your toes, because he's moving fast and expects you to keep up. That last part is true for those who want to read about him in Mark's juggernaut gospel.

Luke

Luke is a physician, a man of science. And so it figures that he would write his gospel account with chronological exactness and careful attention to detail. Like his fellow missionary Mark, Luke writes to a larger audience spread throughout the Roman world—Romans, Greeks, Jews—anyone interested in a detailed account of the Perfect Man. His genealogy of Jesus appeals not just to Jews but to everyone, tracing Jesus all the way back to Adam, the grandfather of us all.[1]

Luke's medical background reveals itself in curious ways. He's the only writer to give us a detailed account of Jesus' birth. Christmas pageants would be a bust if not for this obstetrician's record of the nativity. When Peter cut off the soldier's ear during Jesus's arrest, Matthew, Mark, and John leave a question hanging: What happened to the man without an ear? It's the surgeon who tells us that Jesus reaches out and heals the appendage.

Yet this learned man's gospel story doesn't read like a text-book. The author is dedicated to saving lives, and his own compassion illuminates the Savior's in ways not seen in the other gospels. In Luke we find Jesus going out of his way to serve the forgotten in the world. This God-man cries out for justice and mercy, ministers to the poor and oppressed, pays special attention to women and children.

Luke introduces us to a Jesus very much like ourselves—someone who faces temptation, wrestles injustice, gets angry, cries. What's most significant, Luke shows us a Jesus who needs the Father as much as we do. We read of God the Son consulting with his Father, praying, thanking, beseeching, asking for help all the time. If Jesus needs the Father to survive in this world, we must need him all the more.

John

John writes a different gospel altogether. Like Matthew, he's one of the original gang of twelve, an eye-witness to everything he reports. John's gospel is the most "Jewish" of the books, written in a style reminiscent of the Old Testament. John doesn't fuss with genealogies. In his first lines, he proclaims the Word as God himself, the creator of all things. In short: God has no ancestry, so don't bother to check for references. But *saying* that Jesus is God is one thing; proving it is another. John delivers his proof, using names unmistakable in their meaning to Jews: Lamb of God, Son of God, Messiah, King of Israel, Savior of the World, Bread of Life, Living Water, Light of the World, the Vine—and the clincher, "I AM."

The author throws in an important fact in his last verse: His gospel (or any of the others, for that matter) isn't an exhaustive record of everything Jesus did. But clearly, it's all we need to know to decide the role of the Savior in our own lives.

Acts

Acts is Dr. Luke's sequel to his gospel account, telling what happened when Jesus departs. Like his first work, Acts covers the story chronologically: After the resurrection, Jesus appears to the disciples and tells them he's got to go but will send in the Holy Spirit as his substitute. No mistaking the Spirit's arrival. Ten days after Jesus' ascension, the Spirit comes upon the disciples like a thunderous rush of wind. It rocks the house where they're staying, sending the neighborhood over to investigate.

The disciples begin praising God in foreign languages, which delights the foreigners in the crowd. Others attribute their polyglot performance to excessive wine tasting. Peter steps up to preach his first sermon to the impromptu audience. He concludes with an altar call that brings 3000 new members into the church—a big opening day.

The rest of the book covers the activities of the growing church: miracles and messages, prayers and persecutions, Ananias and Sapphira, the stoning of Stephen, preaching and church planting far and wide, and the conversion and mission trips of Paul. Luke may be the author, but Acts reads like Mark. In the power of the Holy Spirit, the church is on the move.

Wherever the Holy Spirit goes, great power and miracles follow. It's as if Jesus is still around ... but working through his followers. The church flourishes. It doesn't look like a synagogue; it looks more like a hospital. And the sick keep coming. Even enemies of Jesus are converted, Paul among them.

There are growth pains: arrests, persecutions, disbelief, even grumbling among the Christians themselves. But Luke shows us a faith that survives, even grows, in the tough times—a faith that works.

THE NEXT ACT IS OURS

The five books in this section tell an important history, yet they don't finish the gospel story. Jesus shows up, lives, dies, beats the death rap, then returns to heaven. The Holy Spirit shows up, lives in us, and—here's the important part—*he hasn't left us*. The story continues, told in the life of everyone who believes. We must read the Gospels and Acts not as ancient history, but as the first half of a drama in which we play out the finish. Read with a keen eye on the lead Character: How does he speak, think, and act? If he were to play out the part today, what would he do? Study him carefully. Be ready for your cue.

Wait, it gets better: Jesus himself cast you to play your part. Listen in on his conversation with the Director: "As you have sent me into the world, I have sent them into the world" (John 17:18). The Father sent the Son into the world as human, to tell other humans about a loving God. And so he has sent you: as a real live human, to tell other humans about a loving God. No fireworks, no groundshaking—just face, mouth, flesh, blood. And belly button.

LESSON OF THE DAY

See God with a belly button—then study
his role. It's your turn to act it out.

The Letters: From Paul

Read Your Mail

Unlike the disciples, Paul didn't meet Jesus till after Jesus' ascension. Acts tells the story of his encounter with God, which converted him from Christianity's number-one enemy into its most outspoken proponent. Paul planted churches throughout the Roman world, encouraged these churches in their struggles, and wrote *lots* of letters to keep the gospel train rolling.

In a sense, the New Testament's writers were like the Old Testament's prophets. But unlike the prophets, who often spoke face-to-face with the recipients of the hard truth, Paul and his fellow correspondents communicated the truth by mail. But whether in person or on paper, each class of writers often said what people didn't want to hear. Check out Paul as he speaks this kind of truth: **Read *Galatians 3:1–5*.**

His readers were acting as though their good deeds were what most mattered with God. He sets the record straight: "You foolish Galatians! We are justified by faith."

However, from salutation to signature, Paul and his associates couch their letters in love—not to be nice guys or to win writing awards but to draw the far-flung Church together for growth toward Jesus. As Paul himself stated: "Speaking the truth in love, we will in all things grow up into him who is the Head, that is, Christ" (Ephesians 4:15).

PAUL'S CORRESPONDENCE FILE

The New Testament contains 21 letters, grouped by their authors. Paul wrote 13 of them, so he gets to go first. All his letters are titled according to their destination. The first nine are addressed to churches spread across the Roman world. The last four letters are written to individuals. Here's the file.

Romans

Romans is Paul's letter to the educated believers in the pagan capital city. He writes a brilliant explanation of the gospel. There's perfect God, corrupt humans, and just one way for the two to get together: faith in Jesus. His clear, systematic theology has become the model for faith sharing ever since.

1 Corinthians

First Corinthians is Paul's response to a list of questions he received from the church in Corinth, in what is now Greece. We don't have a copy of their letter, but Paul's answers tell us their theme: "How do we live as Christians in a godless, corrupt society?" The problems surrounding them had crept into the church: incest, adultery, mistreatment of the poor, misuse of spiritual gifts. Paul replies with strong rebukes and directives, couched in the kind of love he describes in chapter 13—the letter's most famous passage.

2 Corinthians

Second Corinthians continues the correspondence between Paul and the Corinth church. His previous letter stung them deeply, and they let him know. In his touching reply, Paul confesses that the feeling was mutual: "For I wrote you out of great distress and anguish of heart and with many tears, not to grieve you but to let you know the depth of my love for you" (2:4). The letter is more personal and positive than his last one, containing teachings on joy, giving, and an account of Paul's own real-world struggles.

Galatians

Galatians is written to several churches spread throughout the region of Galatia in Turkey. Paul had visited the region earlier and was later disheartened to learn that they were getting caught up in Jewish traditions rather than the graceful teachings of Christ. As we saw earlier, he lets them know the error of their ways.[1]

Ephesians

Ephesians is written while Paul is stuck behind bars in Rome, to the church stuck smack in the middle of the sex goddess Diana's glitzy hometown of Ephesus, near the Turkish coast. Paul emphasizes the role of the church as the body and bride of Christ. It's a short and positive letter, with lots of great pictures: "the riches of his glorious inheritance" (1:18); "we are God's workmanship" (2:10); "put off your old self" (4:22); "do not give the devil a foothold" (4:27). See for yourself.

Philippians

Philippians is Paul's thank-you note to the believers in Philippi, in what is now northern Greece. He had started this church years earlier—his first European congregation. The church members heard that their founder was doing time in

Rome and sent him a touching gift. This is Paul's most personal letter: He frankly declares "to live is Christ, to die is gain" (1:21); vows to "press on toward the goal" (3:14); and encourages his faithful friends to "shine like stars . . . as you hold out the word of life" (2:15–16).

Colossians

Colossians is another prison letter, sent to the church in Colossae, 100 miles inland of Ephesus. The Colossians are into some strange stuff, practicing a smorgasbord faith that includes Christianity with helpings of Jewish legalism, Oriental mysticism, and Greek philosophy. Paul reminds them that Christ, and Christ alone, is the head of the church. Jesus is not a theology or doctrine: He's a person. And by the way, he's God.

1 Thessalonians

First Thessalonians is Paul's first letter to the church in the Greek city of Thessalonica, an address that barely fit on his stationery. He founded this church on his second mission trip, right after getting things going up in Philippi. Unfortunately, he got run out of town for stealing members from the synagogue, leaving rookie Timothy at the helm (see Acts 17). The young pastor catches up with Paul later in Corinth, and he brings good news: The new church is going strong. Paul sends this letter to commend the church, encourage their walk in Christ, answer questions, deal with problems they're having, and tell them what will happen when Jesus comes back. He hits this last topic a lot.

2 Thessalonians

Second Thessalonians is like the letters to the Corinthians; it's got answers to questions sent in by the church. After reading his first letter, some of the church members got a bit overeager on the Second Coming idea, quitting their jobs and maxing out their credit cards so they could be first in line for the final show. Paul clears up the confusion about Christ's return and tells the idlers to quit embarrassing the church. As in the first letter, he's kind and encouraging, affirming the faithful for their steadfastness under persecution.

1 Timothy

First Timothy is the first of Paul's three pastoral letters, written not to a church but to a minister in its service. Timothy is Paul's young protégé, a dedicated partner on his mission trips. Paul counted on him extensively to support and expand the churches they planted. Paul's first letter to Tim is filled with encouragement: "Fight the good fight" with passion and perseverance. Also enclosed: pastoral guidelines regarding leadership and finances, and procedures for ministry to various groups in the church.

2 Timothy

Second Timothy is even more personal than the first. Paul is back in prison and knows he won't be getting out alive. "I have fought the good fight, I have finished the race, I have kept the faith" (4:7). And now with joy, confidence, and a little sadness too, Paul passes the torch to Timothy. After reading this short letter, you'll want that torch.

Titus

Titus is another young pastor and a dear friend to Paul. He's in charge of the church in Crete. Like his first note to Timothy, Paul's letter to Titus gives instructions on teaching methods and topics, selecting effective leaders for the church—all punctuated with plenty of encouragement.

Philemon

Philemon is a slaveholder, a member of the Colossian church, and someone Paul personally led to the Lord. Paul writes to him on behalf of Onesimus, who had escaped from this master and stolen some stuff in the process. In a stroke of divine irony, Paul runs into the fugitive in Rome and leads him to Christ. Now Paul is in prison, pleading for the convert's life. He even offers to repay Philemon for what Onesimus stole. This very personal letter reveals the writer's deep sense of justice and mercy. Rather than condemn slavery, Paul calls upon this slaveowner (and all others who were to read the letter) to treat a Christian slave not as property but as a brother . . . then leaves the reader to decide what that means for the evil institution of slavery.

TAKE IT PERSONALLY

Paul's letters are easy to read because they're . . . well . . . *letters*. In each, the writer is speaking not to "them" or to people in general but to "you"—second-person, personal, active voice.

And so we should read him that way. Imagine he's writing to *you*. When he says "foolish Galatians" read it as "foolish *Americans*" . . . or *Canadians*, *Presbyterians*, *college students*, *accountants*—whatever fits. When Paul says he's praying "that your love may abound more and more in knowledge and depth of insight," believe that he is. He's the kind of guy who won't let his plush heavenly digs distract him from his daily prayers. And when he writes, "You then, my son, be strong in the grace that is in Christ Jesus," swap the gender if necessary, but don't miss his point. He's talking to you.

LESSON OF THE DAY

Read your mail. The Bible's letters
were written to you.

DAY 16

The Letters: From Others

Keep the Chain Mail Going

The apostle Paul was a prolific correspondent, but not the only one. Jesus' half brother James wrote one, Peter wrote a pair. John wrote three (in addition to his gospel account and Revelation). Jude, another half brother of Jesus, wrote the last letter in the collection. The writer of Hebrews is a mystery . . . something to ask God when we see him.

Paul's letters are titled according to their destination, as is Hebrews. The rest of the Bible's letters are titled by author and numbered when the author had more than one thing to say. Here's the rest of the letter stack.

Hebrews

Hebrews is an unsigned letter. Most likely it was aimed at Jewish Christians living somewhere abroad who were considering reverting to Judaism. The writer uses over 80 Old Testament references to argue that Christ is "greater than Moses," "better than the angels," "the high priest forever," the "sacrifice for all time." The letter shatters their reasons for returning to the obsolete Judaic observances.

James

James almost didn't make it into the Bible, partly because it contains teachings on works that some folks saw as contradictory to the gospel of grace. Careful reading reveals this isn't so, which is what the church fathers decided back in A.D. 397. This fact, along with their belief that Jesus' half brother was almost surely its author, clinched it. The letter is written to Christians everywhere. Like Jesus, James preaches a practical faith that changes how we live: joy in trials, obedience, discipline in speech, prayer, trust, and patience. Sort of a Sermon on the Mount reunion tour.

1 Peter

First Peter is the most famous disciple's first letter to Christians, who are now scattered about the Roman world and suffering persecution. He writes from the capital of that world, as an older, wiser witness to grace than the man who abandoned Jesus in the final hour. He has encouraging words for his embattled brothers and sisters: No matter what your citizenship, job title, marital status, or earthy circumstances, God's grace is sufficient to see you through.

2 Peter

Second Peter is written mere months before the author's execution. Just as false prophets misled the Jews of an earlier day, false teachers among the Christians are spreading confusion and dissension in the church. Peter sends out an advisory to spiritual travelers, showing them how to identify these false teachers, where they err, and how their words depart from the true faith.

1 John

First John is the first of three short letters penned by "the disciple whom Jesus loved." He's an old man now, writing to his "dear children" in the faith, in the same vivid style he used in his gospel: "God is light," so we should "walk in the light"; "God is love" and "lives in us" so "love one another." Like his favorite Teacher, this old pupil shares the truth in words even a child can understand.

2 John

Second John is written to the "chosen lady," either a particular church or an actual woman—he doesn't say. It's more of an e-mail message than a letter, making it the shortest book in the Bible. John returns to his favorite theme of love, warns the reader of false teachers, and explains what to do if you come upon one: Show him the door.

3 John

Third John is a hair longer than his previous note, but this time John names names: Gaius, the recipient; Demetrius, who likely delivered the letter; and Diotrephes, a snooty, inhospitable gossiper whom John intends to confront on his next visit. This is important because Diotrephes is a leader and John doesn't want people to catch his bad habits. Even in slamming the man, John manages to be positive: Love, truth, joy, and peace aren't just words from this old writer; they define his faith.

Jude

Jude, like James, is half brother to Jesus. His letter is to all believers, warning of false teachers and encouraging his readers to "contend for the faith." As other letters have made clear, false teachers, especially Gnostics, are plaguing the church with their perversion of the gospel. Jude deposits them in the same heap as Sodom and Gomorrah, destined for the same fiery future (conveniently described in the very next book). He ends his letter—and the entire collection with it—in a resounding Amen.

CHAIN LETTERS

As we covered yesterday, Paul's letters are meant to be taken personally. Today's collection is no different. The writers wanted their recipients to read, copy, and pass their letters around. It's a good thing they did, because we can't find the originals. Instead, we've got copies, recorded in different hands and languages but all saying the same thing. We know what these writers said the first time because they made sure it got repeated.

So keep these ancient chain letters going. Here's how: First, *make copies.* When you read a passage that hits home with you, don't seal it back up in the book. Write it down. Keep it in your face till you know it by heart.

Second, *distribute.* Don't just read it; do what it says. Act on the words hourly, daily—bring them to life in your world..

Third, *repeat the above.* Take down your note and put it somewhere else. Then find a new passage to copy and distribute.

This simple strategy teaches you to take it personally. That's because as you read, your eye quickly catches the passages that will make sense to you when they stand on their own. Those are the ones meant for you *right now.*

Read the letters *as if* they're written especially to you, and you'll discover a curious thing: They are.

LESSON OF THE DAY

Keep the chain mail going. Copy and distribute God's most important messages.

Revelation

Prepare for the Real Thing

The previous six sections of the Bible contain several books each. The final section contains just one book: Revelation. It's the New Testament's own prophetical section. But it's more than that. Revelation combines poetry, prophecy, and history into a spectacular picture of the world from God's point of view. That's a *big* view—not easily perceived by mere humans—which accounts for much of the disagreement over what this book really means.

On this fact there is no disagreement: God wins in the end. Satan, who made his first appearance not three pages into the story that started back in Genesis, is finally defeated, and Jesus rules unchallenged for the rest of eternity.

The details of the final battle are hard to describe. John rose to the challenge by providing 300 vivid symbols: pictures of things we *do* know to help us form an understanding of what we cannot fully know. His pictures are vivid: lampstand, eagle, lion, lamb, scroll, and so on. We know what these things look like, so he uses them to describe what we've never seen. What's really mindboggling is that we have the play-by-play account of a showdown that hasn't even happened yet! Taken together, these two conditions present both writer and reader with a monumental challenge: How to make sense of things.

THE STORY IN PICTURES

Revelation is actually a letter "to the seven churches in the province of Asia," that is, the churches in what is now Turkey. John is celebrating the Lord's Day on the Mediterranean island of Patmos (about forty miles off the coast of Turkey) when a loud voice comes up from behind and instructs him to write down everything he's about to see, then to send the transcript to the churches. He turns around to see a sharply-dressed man holding an even sharper sword in his mouth and seven stars in his hand, and standing among seven gold lampstands. The man identifies himself as "the First and the Last"; this and other hints tell us this revelation is from Christ himself. Just like in the old days, Jesus is the real storyteller; his friend John just writes it down.

First Christ tells him to record a message to each of the seven churches, which he identifies by name. The names may have changed (unless you happen to live in Philadelphia), but church conditions haven't—the messages describe good and bad stuff happening in churches then and now.

Then, John's vision dissolves to an exterior shot of heaven, door open—and a voice beckoning him inside. Cut to an interior, dominated by a rainbow-wrapped throne, with Someone on it. Then two dozen lesser thrones, all occupied, and four strange winged creatures, and everyone worshiping the Someone in the middle, who's God Almighty.

The vision zooms to a closeup of God's right hand grasping a scroll shut tight with seven seals. "Who is worthy to break the seals and open the scroll?" thunders a nearby angel. John weeps when he learns that no one in heaven or on earth can be found for the job. Tears turn to joy when someone next to him speaks: "See, the Lion of the tribe of Judah, the Root of David, has triumphed. He is able to open the scroll and its seven seals" (5:5).

On cue, Jesus appears in the form of the Lamb, snatches the scroll from his enthroned Father's hand, and starts snapping seals. What happens next? In short, hell breaks loose. Satan launches into a spine-chilling sequence of horrors, each more wicked than the last. His crime spree starts in chapter 6 and continues till his arrest in chapter 20.

THE PRINCIPAL PLAYERS

A lot goes on in these chapters, and most of it in groups of seven: seals, angels, trumpets, thunders, thousands, heads, crowns, plagues, bowls. Also marching in this parade of sevens are many key characters, some with multiple names. Here's a roster to help you sort them out.

God's Side

There's God the Father himself, who pretty much stays on the heavenly throne, so he's not hard to follow. Then there's Jesus, who appears as the Lamb, a newborn child, "the son of a man," "Lord of lords and King of kings," and as a rider on a white horse. In the heaven scenes, 24 "elders" sit on lesser thrones around God's or fall on the floor to worship him. These scenes also feature four multiwinged creatures: One looks like a lion, another like a calf, a third has a face like a man, and the fourth like a flying eagle.[1]

Of course there are plenty of angels too, including the chief angel Michael (whom Jude calls "archangel"). Down on earth there are two "witnesses" who, like the old prophets, tell the people what they don't want to hear. When the crowd has heard all they can stand, they kill the two witnesses and celebrate in the streets of Jerusalem. The festivities are interrupted three and a half days later when the two witnesses come back to life. The resurrected witnesses ascend to heaven in a cloud, leaving the incredulous revelers staring at the sky.

Also on God's side is a very pregnant woman dressed in sunny clothes and a twelve-starred crown. She gives birth to a boy, so you can figure her for Israel. She has other children who play key roles—prophets and apostles, "the 144,000," the saints (Christians)—who all become the bride of Christ (the church).

Other Side

Satan shows up as a seven-headed, star-sweeping dragon, whom John also calls the Serpent and the Devil. Then there's "the beast"—mostly like a leopard, with feet like a bear and a mouth like a lion . . . and seven heads, giving us a clue as to whose call it heeds. (His popular name is the antichrist, but John uses that name only in his first letter.) The beast and his master are a big hit with those who don't follow Jesus. People worship the demonic duo and do as they're told—which includes inflicting misery and murder on the faithful.

Then there's *another* creature, this one with lamblike horns and a dragonlike voice, a.k.a. "the false prophet." This guy is a universal sensation: He performs spectacular miracles and forces everyone to get a tattoo of the beast's insidious logo. It seems he's the charismatic spokesperson for the antichrist in the evil government of the last days. This political system is called Babylon, which John sees as a giant prostitute. Her clients are the kings and commoners who bow to the system. Satan also has evil angels and demons schlepping for him.

THE MILLENNIUM

The above cast acts out a complicated series of events that's hard to understand. Scholars have been trying to make sense of it for years, and there's still much disagreement regarding what will really happen and the order in which it will take place. Some scenes appear to have taken place already: The heavenly battle between the dragon and Michael (chapter 12) looks a lot like Ezekiel's description of Satan's primordial downfall. But maybe not.

Even the tribulation—the troubled days before the final day—is difficult to define. Some folks believe that Christians will be snatched up before things turn nasty. Others see relief coming in the middle of the mess. Still others say believers will be in it for the duration. It depends on whose book you read.

This much is clear: In chapter 19, Christ returns to fight a victorious battle over Satan and his evil forces. Take a peek at the big entrance scene: **Read *Revelation 19:11–16*.**

In the next chapter, Satan is thrown in jail for a thousand years while Christ reigns in peace. At the end of his sentence, Satan is released. Like a duck on a June bug (my vision, not John's), he returns to make war. Amazingly, after ten centuries of peace, countless humans are still eager to enlist on Satan's side.

God puts a stop to it all by casting Satan and his cronies into hell for ever and ever. Then the Lord passes a similar judgment on those who chose Satan as their master, sending these rebel troops straight to their commander's permanent headquarters. Finally, God wipes the universal slate clean and starts fresh: a brand-new heaven and earth. This unblemished world includes a new Jerusalem, constructed of gold and jewels—a pretty fine place for the saints who will live there forever.

The book and John's vision ends with words of comfort and warning, and a guarantee that Christ will indeed return for his people: "Yes, I am coming soon." To which John replies, "Amen. Come, Lord Jesus." And so we wait.

FUTURE ENJOYMENT

Reading Revelation challenges the skills you've learned in other Bible sections. It contains history (of the past *and* the future), so enjoy it that way: Test the good parts in your own life to duplicate the results. The specific messages to the seven churches in chapters 2 and 3 provide excellent research data.

There's plenty of poetry, which reads best when you form the pictures in your head. This is essential in Revelation because most of John's word pictures are incomprehensible in the literal sense. Remember that he's describing governments and technology and weapons of war that didn't exist in his day. Use your modern-day imagination to ponder what he *might* have been describing.

And first to last, it's prophecy. God told Isaiah that Jesus was coming, then delivered as promised. This same God told John that Jesus was *coming back*. Are we seeing a pattern here? In both cases the prophecies even name the arrival gate: Last time he arrived in a Bethlehem barn; next time he's showing up in grand style, for all the world to see. Here's the clincher: We don't know the arrival time.

Through the old prophets, God sent his people important messages that affected their future. Through John's vision, the same God has sent us a life-or-death alert: *Christ is coming back. Be ready!*

Remember those fire drills back at school? The buzzers would sound, the students would scurry, and the principal would stand outside with a stopwatch to measure our readiness. We never knew if it was the real thing. But we were ready ... just in case.

Read Revelation as if you're going through a fire drill. When the buzzers go off (actually, they're trumpets now), will you be ready? Is your life in order? Are you properly packed? What's your escape route? (Hint: There's only one.) Because one of these days, it *won't* be a drill. And those who aren't prepared will perish in the flames.

Are you confused by Revelation's prophetic details? You're in the company of countless others. Do the horrific visions frighten you? Me too—that's why we hold hands. Are you unsure about what to do to survive? It's simple: Get right with God through Jesus—he's the only one who can rescue you from the trouble ahead. Call out, "Come, Lord Jesus!" And he will. Immediately, in the spirit. And soon, in the flesh.

LESSON OF THE DAY

Prepare for the real thing: Jesus will return. Be ready to greet him face to face.

PART THREE

How to Read It

DAY 18

"It's Inaccurate"

Read Like You're Looking at the First Edition

How do we know that the Bible is accurate? Some people are surprised to learn that we have not a single original document for the 66 books. It doesn't matter. We can still test the accuracy of the copies we've got. Most of the Bible's major events were recorded by more than one witness. This is true in the Old Testament and especially so in the New. We can confirm the accuracy of one writer's account by examining the testimony of other witnesses.

But as any lawyer will tell you, corroborating stories can be fabricated if the alleged witnesses swap answers before the trial. Did the Bible writers conspire to write matching stories? If so, they were either extremely stupid or smarter than God. Their stories match, but they're not identical. Many Old Testament events are recorded in two sets of history books plus the prophets, yet each tells the story differently. The gospels often give us four accounts of the same episode. In each case the testimony varies in style, language, context, and attention to detail. At times the variations are so great that they almost cast doubt on the testimony. If these were written by coconspirers, they didn't do a very clean job.

But maybe they were smarter than that. Maybe they purposely inserted the variations to throw us off track—to make us *think* that each wrote independently of the others. That's possible but highly unlikely. In many cases the witnesses never met. Like dandelion seeds in a windstorm, the Jews were seasonally scattered throughout the Middle East and Mediterranean through wars and persecutions. Filing their reports from separate locations, they often had no way to guess what the others would say.

For those who still have doubts, we call up the expert witnesses—people who didn't see the events but can attest to their accuracy. The first expert is the ancient Jews themselves. They took God's word very seriously. To forget the past was to doom themselves to repeat it. They learned that lesson the hard way . . . and many times over. The best way to keep track of their history was to write it down and make accurate copies for safekeeping. Each generation took the books of the past, added their own books, and passed the collection to the next generation. Centuries before Christ they had accumulated all the books we now call the Old Testament, and considered them the sacred word of God.

The Jews had incessant scrapes with other nations, so we can also look to their histories for corroboration. Persian, Greek, Roman, and other foreign historians record key moments in Jewish history, especially of the wars fought and battles won. The conspiracy theory goes out the window when these outside experts take the stand.

Of course, Christians are more concerned about the accuracy of the New Testament. The best case for its accuracy is the sheer volume of early manuscripts still in existence. As we discussed earlier, Jesus gave the disciples a directive: Spread the Good News! They did so immediately. Ironically, their enemies helped them. The Jewish religious leaders were eager to stamp out the upstart Christian movement and raised a ruckus (and a rock-fest in Stephen's case) to do it. The Roman government didn't want troublemakers either, so together they helped scatter the disturbance—that is, the church. As the contagious Christians moved elsewhere, they infected their new neighbors. The faith spread like an epidemic throughout the Roman Empire.

With believers spread around the Mediterranean, the only way to keep in touch and on the right faith track was through writing. We can thank God that they didn't have phones back then, because their written testimonies and correspondence provide us with the entire New Testament.

We don't have those original notes and letters today, nor do we have their immediate copies. But we have so many later copies that it doesn't matter. Right now there are *thousands* of manuscripts dating from the early centuries of the church stored in libraries and vaults around the world. These books, letters, notes, and fragments were found in various distant places, written in many languages, at different times—yet they agree in content. Had the first Christians hidden out in a persecution-proof compound, we'd have little or nothing to define our faith—that is, if we had any faith at all.

SAMPLE A FIRST EDITION

You can find many good books that discuss the accuracy of the Bible. Ask your pastor or Christian bookseller to recommend titles if you want to learn more. You may even find helpful information on the Bible's proofs and publication history in the front or back of your own Bible. The *best* proof of the Bible is presented not in scholarly arguments but in the evidence of your own life.

Way back in Day 6 we explored the idea that the Bible is a collection of research data: the results of ancient experiments in faith. Our task is to reenact the best experiments to see if we can duplicate the results. We were talking specifically about Bible history, but the whole book works that way. You can prove its accuracy by testing its message on yourself. Paul himself makes this bold claim: **Read 2 *Timothy* 3:16–17.**

That's a dangerous passage. Paul, a formidable Bible scholar and former skeptic to Christ's teachings, asserts that all Scripture is "God-breathed" (can anything *be* more accurate?) and "useful" for real-life experimentation. Look closely and you can almost hear him whisper, "So try it. *I dare you.*"

As you read Scripture, take the dare. If you come upon something that taunts your belief, take God's promise for a test-drive. See for yourself if the writers knew what they were talking about. Because the One who breathed life into the first edition is still alive and puffing, eager to breath new life into you.

LESSON OF THE DAY

Read like you're looking at the first edition.
The Author is ready to prove its accuracy
through a personal demonstration.

"It's Old"

Read Like It Was Written Today

In the Archives Building in Washington, D.C., inside a bulletproof, fireproof, bombproof display, you'll find the original Constitution of the United States. The parchment is faded, the type is rough and uneven, and the last page is sprinkled with inky signatures of the lawyers and farmers who argued it into existence. It's an impressive piece of 18th-century history.

But more impressive is the evidence of that old document, everywhere you look. Every day in America, attorneys, judges, police officers, criminals, citizens—in short, *all* Americans—rely upon the words printed on those old pages to "secure the Blessings of Liberty." In a society that measures the staying power of news in days, the popularity of books in weeks, where relationships are measured in months and clothing styles in seasons, it's supremely strange that after 200 years the Constitution is still in fashion. The question is, why? The answer for most of us is simple: It's still true. Or to put it another way, it's as true today as it was when it was written. That's the measure of real truth: It works without a calendar. You've already guessed where I'm headed here, so let's just get on with it.

THE BIBLE IS TRUE FOR ALL TIME

Real, timeless truth is hard to come by. Culture and technology change so quickly that last year's fashion statement becomes this year's clown suit; today's computer is next year's doorstop. The latest miracle diet, painless exercise plan, or self-help scheme is soon discovered to hurt more than it helps. And yesterday's news is ... well, yesterday's news. Most of what we humans come up with turns out to be flash-in-the-pan fads—here today, trash tomorrow.

The problem comes down to perspective. If we could *see* the past and the present and the future all at once, we'd know what was good and workable and true for all these times. But on our own we're stuck in the here and now, with a sketchy picture of the past and nothing but psychic hotlines to misguide our future.

That's where God sure comes in handy. According to him (and he ought to know), he's the inventor of time. He stands above our clocks and calendars and sees what's going on in all of time, all the time. But don't take my word for it—check it out for yourself. **Read** *Acts 17:24–26.*

It's nice to know that God has a timeless perspective of life here on planet Earth. That means he's able to give us timeless truths. But that doesn't mean he *has to*. Maybe he throws in some faddish truths, just to be fashionable with the people he's speaking to at the time. Like all those old people in the Bible. How else (you ask) can you explain stories like the one found in *1 Chronicles 4:9–10*? Good question! Let's take a look at these verses.

At first glance this tiny story seems like a useless tidbit of ancient history. In the middle of someone's family tree, we find a guy with a funny name who's not too thrilled about it. Big deal, right? Well, it is a big deal if your name is Jabez! Parents name their kids for all sorts of things—famous people (George Washington Carver), character traits (Hope, Faith), natural phenomenon (Sitting Bull), and who-knows-what (Moon Unit Zappa). How did your parents come up with *your* name?

Jabez knew where his name came from. Like many Jews, his name made a *statement*: His came from the Hebrew word for pain. Now, that's some statement. As you just read, his mother named him Jabez because that sensation was uppermost in her mind while she was in labor. (Maybe she was shouting the word so much that those attending her wrote it on the birth certificate by mistake; the text doesn't say.) But if every woman named her baby the way this mother did, we'd all be named either Jabez or Epidural.

You can imagine Jabez's first day at school. It would have been the same as your first day—had your folks named you something like Pain-in-the-Butt. A name like that is a self-fulfilling prophecy, drawing pain and ridicule and sorrow to its owner—who then inflicts his namesake on everyone around him. As a kid, my own nickname, Trouble, started out as a description but soon became a job title as I sought to live up to what people expected of me.

Okay, so the Jabez story does have relevance today . . . if you've got a bad name. True, but it goes further than that. Names are not the only things we inherit from our folks. Parents can burden their kids with all sorts of pains: divorce, alcoholism, abuse, neglect, overbearance. These handicaps cling tighter than a bad name.

But the story of Jabez shows us that there's hope: Jabez recognized his inherited handicap, and rather than succumb to its destructive power, he prayed to God for the help to overcome it. And God answered. Jabez kept the name but not the baggage that came with it.

When you take a moment to imagine yourself in Jabez's shoes, you discover that the message of this ancient and seemingly useless story is timeless: God can rescue us from pain we inherit from our parents. That's good news today, whatever your name is.[1]

WHY HIDE THE TRUTH IN OLD STORIES?

Now, some might say that using stories based on ancient cultures and customs is a confusing way to convey truth. Why didn't God dispense with Jabez and just say that he can help us overcome the sins of our parents? Why didn't he leave out all the old stories and just give us the timeless truths they contain (in the words of Joe Friday, "Just the facts, ma'am")?

Because we'd have a pretty sorry-reading Bible, that's why. Imagine excising the characters and stories from any good book: What would *Huckleberry Finn*, or *Kidnapped*, or *A Christmas Carol* (to name a few of my favorites) look like if the authors had just stuck with the messages behind these great stories? Huck Finn would read, "Slavery bad, friendship good, nighttime river navigation dangerous without lights."[2]

An entire Bible without characters and stories would read like . . . well, like certain sections of Leviticus. (Don't worry, we won't be going there today.) When the message is delivered through real, live characters, in real-world circumstances, the truth is not only more enjoyable to read, it's *safer*—you can see what it does to other humans before trying it on yourself.

Something else. The more difficult the story, the harder we must work our brains and hearts to find the truth it contains—and the more we must rely upon the Holy Spirit to give us hints. That's a good thing, because we most treasure what we discover for ourselves. Ask any veteran of an Easter egg hunt. Or read Proverbs 2 (on your own time—we're onto something else right now).

READ THE BIBLE AS IF IT WERE WRITTEN TODAY

Now, if God knows the timeless truths and he's revealed these timeless truths in the Bible, the conclusion is simple: The Bible is filled with truths for today. Which means you really can read it as if it were written just hours ago, its ink still wet with relevance. Here's how.

Talk to the Author

Before you read, ask the Holy Spirit for hints. Unlike the authors of most great books, who are either dead, distant, or keep unlisted phone numbers, you can speak to the Author of this great Book. Ask him to help you discover the timeless truths—the message that's meant for you *today*.

Change Your Shoes

When you read, take off your shoes and wear a pair from someone who was there at the time. In other words, place yourself in that world, at that time, and try to imagine what you might be seeing, hearing, feeling, wanting, needing. You've been doing this all your life: In *The Cat in the Hat* and ghost tales at camp, through novels and news stories and feature films, you've identified with the characters and lived the stories in their shoes. It's not hard if you try.

Retie Your Shoes

If the truth is timeless, it can apply to your life today. What does your world now look like in light of this truth? Does the truth change your perspective? Does it help you understand a situation, problem, or challenge you're facing right now? Read it as if it were written today.

Retell the Story

You're one of the fortunate few who's read the original piece. For the sake of those around you who haven't, retell the story in your own life. If the message in the original is timeless, it'll make a great modern version when you live it today. Act today *as if* this were true. You'll discover, as will those around you, that God's word is still alive and kicking.

LESSON OF THE DAY

Read like it was written today.
This truth is timeless—true
yesterday, today, and tomorrow.

"It's Morally Confusing"

Read Like It's Written by the Definition of Good

When I was a kid, I had a pristine view of the Bible. I hadn't really read it, but I had a pretty good idea of what it was about: God, sin, right, wrong, squeaky-clean morals, and dirty consequences for those who don't obey. My understanding of the Bible's contents supported my moral code, which could be summed up as, *don't lie, don't steal, obey your parents*, and *be nice*. (I failed miserably, by the way.)

It wasn't until I was a teenager that I actually took longer jaunts in the Bible. I found lots of great stuff in there but plenty of disturbing passages too. My moral code had expanded by then to include, among other things, *treat women and men equally*. You can imagine my dismay when I opened the Bible only to learn that the ancients—*God's* people—didn't support my own views on equality!

And the more I read in this Book, the more disturbing it gets. The ancients fail to obey my taboos on war, slavery, racism, environmental destruction, and animal cruelty. Page after page, God's people offend my sense of right and wrong, and often do so with God's implicit blessing—or at his outright command. Okay, I'm ready to be totally frank: Certain parts of this moral book seem downright *immoral*!

Here's the worst part: I'm not the only one who has noticed. Critics often blame the Bible for perpetuating these evils. After all, American slaveholders used Scripture to defend their institution, opponents of women's suffrage did the same, and today as I write this, some believer somewhere is quoting a Bible verse to rationalize something the rest of us know is wrong.

Which leads many of us to ask, Why didn't God teach, practice, and uphold right from wrong? Well, as I've come to learn, he did. But he went about it in his own strange way. Let's look at one of his most confusing moral judgments. **Read *Deuteronomy 7:1–2.***

Moses is repeating God's marching orders to the Israelites prior to their invasion of Canaan: When you come upon the current inhabitants, "destroy them totally." Annihilate. Wipe them out. There are no two ways about it: God was sanctioning genocide.

We cringe when we read this verse and many others like it. We edit such passages from our Sunday school lessons to protect our kids from the blood-curdling truth. And privately we wonder how the Author of love can be so mean. Our moral conscience battles with our faith. It's an unnerving experience because we thought these two things were on the same side.

The answer comes only when both sides surrender. We have to give up trying to make God in our image, stop insisting that he conform to our moral standards. We have to throw in the towel and let God be God—with the privileges that come with the title: absolute justice, perfect love, ultimate sovereignty.

Let's wave our white flags while we look at this passage again: Was God unfair in demanding the death of the Canaanites? No, he's absolutely just. He knew their hearts, he knew their plans—apparently, they were unredeemable. What about innocent children—did he damn them to hell? Impossible. That would be unjust, and God doesn't dabble with injustice.

When God wields a sword, he strikes with perfect aim. He's the only one who can. The trouble starts when we amateurs try to do it on our own. We hit the wrong people and always cut ourselves in the process. There are many godly attributes he wants us to emulate, but sword-juggling is not one of them.

Did God sanction the Jews to commit genocide on the people of Canaan? Yes. But it was *God's* decision, *God's* justice, *God's* sword, not theirs. Did this act give us all a license to kill? No. God himself makes it clear: "It is mine to avenge; I will repay" (Deuteronomy 32:35).

In other words, God was saying, "Do as I say, not as I do." It sounds hypocritical when put like that, but it's true. Parents do things that their young kids shouldn't try, like drive, vote, drink, have sex, and work twelve-hour days. Certain privileges (and pains) come with age and wisdom. As the oldest and wisest among us, God is qualified for things off-limits to his children. "Obey me," he says, "*I'll* tell you what's right." When the children of Israel obeyed their Dad, things went great. When they played dressup and acted as if they were God, pretending to possess all the rights and privileges thereof, they were punished. Father knows best.

In the Old Testament God had one overriding moral ground rule: "Do as I say." In the New Testament he adds an important line: "Do as I say ... *AND as I do*." Jesus sets aside his parental privileges, puts away his divine driver's license, and *shows* us how to live as children of the Father. He says "love your enemies," and he does it. To be forgiven, you must forgive. He forgives. If you want to be first, you must make yourself a servant. And so he does. In Jesus we have a God not just to be obeyed but to be emulated. He *shows* us what's right, through a personal demonstration.

Still, some complain that Christ's teachings and doings weren't specific enough. He could have sped up women's rights two millennia simply by appointing women to his disciple board. And while he was flipping flea market tables at his Father's house, why didn't he invite the rest of the world to this Jews-only party? For that matter, why didn't he free his own people from the Roman oppressors? Any of these moral stands could have saved us all a lot of trouble.

Jesus *could* have done all these things. And if he had, we'd still be sitting here, struggling with whatever moral issues he left out. So instead of addressing each right and every wrong, Christ covered them all in short order: "Love the Lord your God with all your heart and with all your soul and with all your strength and with all your mind; and, Love your neighbor as yourself" (Luke 10:27). Then he leaves Christians in all circumstances, cultures, and eras to figure out what that means for them.

In light of this teaching, can a slaveowner justify his behavior? I don't see how. Can a man justify the abuse or oppression of a woman? Not according to Jesus. Can any of us rationalize racism, greed, hatred, cruelty, injustice, or apathy? You figure it out. We Christians may confuse the truth for our own selfish gain, but the confusion is ours, not God's.

God's morality is fit for human consumption; as proof, Jesus tested it on himself. His teachings contain timeless moral principles that work in the real world, then and now. In the first century women were property. Jesus treats them like people. Children were workhorses. Jesus protects them—and says that those who do otherwise are better off dead. The sick and the poor were despised and abused. Jesus treats them with dignity.

Jesus was a revolutionary social activist, even by today's standards. If we have failed to apply his principles to our own social ills, we're the old-fashioned ones, not him.

SQUARE OFF WITH THE MORAL DILEMMAS

The Bible contains many passages that prompt our conscience to cry foul. Most are in the Old Testament, but you'll even find some in the New. It's tempting to skip the offending verses or at least set them aside to sort out later. Don't do it. If a piece of Scripture strikes your moral senses, you're right where you need to be. Take the time to figure out why.

First, confess your complaint. What is it about the story that offends you? Why does it seem wrong? Then sort out the parties: Who's committing the offense? If it's a human, is the culprit acting under God's direct authority or on his or her own agenda? If it's the latter, your conscience is in the clear . . . or maybe it isn't: Compare the sinner's offense to events in your own life. Are you guilty of the same charge? As Jesus says, "First take the plank out of your own eye, and then you will see clearly to remove the speck from your brother's eye" (Matthew 7:5). Moral indignation starts at home.

If the "offender" is someone acting under God's authority, or even God himself, the only thing you can do is surrender. If God is God, he's moral by definition. He makes no mistakes. He does the right thing, at the right time, every time. He's *good*.

That's what Job found out when he asked the Lord why bad things were happening to him. You'll find God's answer in chapters 38 through 41. It's a long answer, so I'll give you a summary: God is all-knowing, all-powerful, all-good. And when in our tiny human minds we can't quite see it that way, we've just got to trust him. It's not easy, but it's the only sensible choice.

There's a bonus blessing to these moral dilemmas: In sorting them out, we get to know God better. He comes out bigger than we thought and even better than we hoped for.

LESSON OF THE DAY

Read like it's written by the Definition of Good—ultimate morality is defined in God's character. Demonstrate that fact by emulating Christ's behavior.

"It's Boring"

Read Something Else!

To most people, the Bible is the longest book they've never read. It's one old, strange, scary, occasionally incomprehensible, often boring, giant, great big book!

Actually, it's not.

It's sixty-six books, all stuck together. I know it's best to publish them in one fat volume, but that's a shame. It's a *collection* of books, after all, and collections read better one at a time. I don't have a set of encyclopedias, but when I use someone else's, I'm thankful the publishers broke them up into the alphabet. I do have the complete works of Charles Dickens. They take up their own bookshelf. I'm glad all Dickens' writings aren't crammed betwixt two covers—I'd never have read them.

I wish I had a similar set of Bible books: Sixty-six volumes, set back to back, the titles on their narrow spines calling out softly, "Read me; I'm short and sweet." Somehow I think I'd get through the whole Bible quicker that way. And I'd surely enjoy it more.

Of course, if the Bible were published only as individual books, I'd complain that it was inconvenient: "Why doesn't someone combine all these volumes into one convenient package?" I guess I'm just hard to please.

SOMETHING ELSE TO READ

If you're like me, your list of excuses for not reading the Bible runs longer than the Big Book itself. But if "boring" is high on your excuse list, there's a great solution: *Read something else.* I don't mean read a different book. I mean read a different Bible. Or read the same Bible in a new way. Try one of the following.

Switch Versions

If you've worn out the pages of your favorite Bible—or reading it over and over has worn you out—give your old friend a vacation and take a spin in a different version. Sometimes a fresh look at an old passage gives it new life. Things look curiously different, and this curiosity pulls you into the text to see what they're saying.

Try a Paraphrase

Reading a paraphrased passage is like listening to a friend tell a story. The storyteller may miss some of the details, but the casual, personal language makes for easy listening; your mind is freed up to enjoy the adventure—even if you've already heard it.

Listen to King James

If this old translation is not your version of choice, try some passages from it. You may be in for a surprise. Reading the KJV is like listening to someone speak with a foreign accent. The speaker constructs sentences and chooses words that force you to listen more carefully. It takes more work on your part to grasp what he's saying, but this work is rewarded with a new understanding of what seemed so plain before.

Change Places

Location is everything. If you're reading the Bible in the same setting every time, try moving to a new reading room—indoors or out—or a new time of day. Routines that start out as disciplines can soon breed boredom. Get out of the rut.

Hear God's Word

Pick up a reading of the Bible on audiotape. Or take turns reading with a spouse, friend, or child. Sometimes it's not the text that gets old; its our own voice we get tired of.

Read It Like a Book

That sounds obvious, but most of us don't read the Bible that way. We make it through a passage or a chapter and call it a day. Pick up the Bible and read one book in a sitting. Pretend it's a volume in your bookshelf collection. When you're done, put it away and pick up a new one.

THE TREASURE

We live in a world where mountains of information fall on us daily, measured in full-color magazine pages, TV minutes, and multimedia megabytes. In comparison, God's Word just sits there, in plain old black and white. But looks are deceiving. We hold in our hands the most interactive information device ever devised. Solomon was one of its inventors, and he described how it works: **Read** *Proverbs 2:1–5*.

Solomon is describing the first-ever, interactive, multimedia-learning adventure game. Here's how to play: Knowledge of God is the world's greatest treasure. God's Word is our treasure map.

If we study this map—listen, read, ponder, ask questions, *apply*—we will discover the treasure. At times this treasure hunt is fun; other times it seems to drag on forever. But it's a great adventure—sometimes in the *reading* but always in the *doing*.

So keep hunting. Keep reading. Keep applying. This is a game you can win. Keep your eye on the Prize.

LESSON OF THE DAY

Read something else—discover what you're missing. Try a new version or environment. A treasure awaits!

POSTSCRIPT

Congratulations! You've done it! You've completed the 21-day trip. Along the way you've sampled the major genres of biblical literature, visited the seven major sections of the Bible, and taken a turn at tackling the nagging questions that may keep you away from Scripture.

Throughout the journey, I've given you simple reading tips and daily lessons to help you jump in and enjoy your reading. I've tried and tested these techniques on myself. If they can work even for me, there's great hope for you!

I used many resources in my own preparations to write this book, including some that may help you enjoy your reading, too. I also asked pastors and teachers and longtime Bible students which resources they've found helpful. Here's a very short list of our favorites.

- Study Bibles (lots of notes and background material to help you sort out the difficult passages)
- Walk Thru the Bible Ministries (great interactive seminars held nationwide, plus helpful followup resources: 770–458–9300)
- *The Message* by Eugene Peterson; NavPress (a delightful modern paraphrase of New Testament, Psalms, and Proverbs)
- *What the Bible Is All About* by Henrietta Mears; Regal (a simple Bible tour from a famous Sunday school teacher)

- *The Book of God* by Walter Wangerin Jr.; Zondervan (the Bible as a single, narrative story, told with dignity and care)
- *NIV Harmony of the Gospels* by Robert L. Thomas and Stanley N. Gundry; Harper and Row (a side-by-side, chronological telling of the four gospels)

Of course there are *hundreds* of Bible-reading resources available, but these stand out for my friends and me. Ask your pastor to recommend (or lend) others that can help you enjoy your reading.

Last tip: Reread *this* book! Not the whole thing. Just review the parts that support your Bible reading. If you're jumping into the Psalms, skim the two chapters on poetry. If you're in the historical books, review those chapters. My thoughts may give you a helping hand and remind you of the reading tricks for these passages.

Thanks for joining me on this wild ride through the Bible. My prayer is that it's been as helpful for you as it's been for me. In the introduction I told you that learning to enjoy your Bible is not a 21-day process but a lifelong journey. I hope this book has been a good start, or a refreshing *re*start, for you. Which means . . .

Keep going! You've got a running start—now use it to enjoy your daily reading. Practice the techniques we've covered and discover some new ones on your own. Ask lots of questions. Listen for the answers. Reenact the experiments. Let the Author write his Word in your life, till it overflows for all to read.

NOTES

Introduction

1. A note to Catholic readers: If you're using a Catholic Bible, you're in for a surprise: This tour is missing some books! That's because it's based on the Protestant Bible, containing the 66 books included in the canon selected by the church fathers at the Council of Carthage back in the year 397.

Your Bible contains seven additional Old Testament books which are not covered on our tour: four Historical books (Tobit, Judith, 1 Maccabees, 2 Maccabees); two Poetical books (Wisdom and Sirach), and one Prophetical book (Baruch). The Catholic Bible also includes extra passages in Esther (chapters A through F) and Daniel (chapters 13 and 14). Your New Testament is identical to the Protestant version.

The 73-book Catholic canon was defined at the Council of Trent in 1546, a decision the Protestant movement rejected. Some Bibles put these and other "extra" books and passages in a section called the Apocrypha. In any case, you're welcome to use your Catholic Bible on the tour; just skip over the books we don't visit. Or pick up a Protestant version if you like—I promise not to tell your priest.

DAY 4: It's Got Poetry

1. For a more modern version of this kind of writing, read Martin Luther King Jr.'s "I Have a Dream" speech. True to his Bible roots (and skillfully paraphrasing from the source), King sets up a poetic rhythm that you can't quite clap to, but you're too busy shouting amens to notice.

DAY 5: It's Got Reality

1. If you're like me, you've already skimmed the next paragraph, figured out that this verse is about David and Bathsheba, and figured, "Why look it up? I already know the story." Well, read it again, because there are some details here we're going to explore. I'll wait.

DAY 9: Historical Books: Joshua to 2 Kings

1. The journey from Egypt to Canaan begins, ends, and depends on bold women who defy civil authority in service to God. Moses' mother started it all with her ingenious floating bassinet. Rahab's rebel work got the spies back safe and sound—had they not returned, the Jews might have turned tail and spent another 40 years learning how to trust God.

DAY 11: Poetical Books

1. This same sensible order is used in the New Testament: history (Gospels and Acts), philosophy (the Letters), and prophecy (Revelation).

DAY 14: The Gospels and Acts

1. As far as we know, Luke's the only non-Jewish writer in the New Testament. He's also the most prolific—his gospel and the book of Acts run longer than Paul's collection of letters. Not even John, with a gospel, three letters, and a revelation, can touch him.

DAY 15: The Letters: From Paul

1. This letter carries a hefty punch: Fifteen centuries after its ink dried, Martin Luther flung it at the church in Rome to defend his argument against their works-weighted doctrines.

DAY 17: Revelation

1. Some readers connect these creatures to the four images of Christ as set forth in the Gospels: Matthew's regal Lion of Judah, Mark's sacrificial servant, Luke's Son of Man, and John's Son of God, soaring in the heavenly realm.

DAY 19: "It's Old"

1. You can read about another Jabez in Ogden Nash's poem "The Boy Who Laughed at Santa Claus." It's the story of one Jabez Dawes, a little boy whose short career was spent in fulfillment of his name: "He stole the milk of hungry kittens, and walked through doors marked No Admittance."

2. Apologies to Mr. Twain, whose own foreword to the book states, Persons attempting to find a motive in this narrative will be persecuted; persons attempting to find a moral in it will be banished; persons attempting to find a plot in it will be shot." But truth sneaks through in any good story, despite the teller's disclaimer.

Available in April 1998:

In *21 Days to a Better Quiet Time with God*, author Timothy Jones shows readers how taking just a few minutes from their day to share with God can enrich their lives immensely.
Softcover 0-310-21749-0

In *21 Days to Better Fitness*, leading health and fitness author Maggie Greenwood-Robinson offers readers a simple, day-by-day strategy for improving their fitness and health.
Softcover 0-310-21750-4

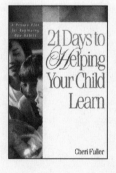

21 Days to Helping Your Child Learn by Cheri Fuller is a short course in teaching kids the joys of thinking creatively and learning naturally.
Softcover 0-310-21748-2

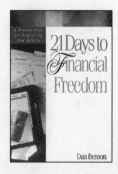

21 Days to Financial Freedom features a simple and practical financial plan that anyone can use, from the series' editor Dan Benson.
Softcover 0-310-21751-2

We want to hear from you. Please send your comments about this book to us in care of the address below. Thank you.

ZondervanPublishingHouse
Grand Rapids, Michigan 49530
http://www.zondervan.com